BRIOCHE KNITTING WORKSHOP

BRIOCHE KNITTING WORKSHOP

A BEGINNER'S GUIDE
TO BRIOCHE TECHNIQUES
WITH 15 MODERN PATTERNS

Lavanya Patricella

DAVID & CHARLES
— PUBLISHING —

www.davidandcharles.com

CONTENTS

38
42
66
88
46
70
92
50
78
98
110
54
58
82
104

FOREWORD

I first met Lavanya during a knitting workshop and Westknits Trunk Show in Philadelphia, and it instantly felt like I was meeting an old friend I had known for years. Lavanya and I quickly bonded over color, fashion, and brioche knitting. I love Lavanya's curious and inquisitive spirit, matched with the passion to share her knowledge and make other people feel confident and comfortable with their knitting. These characteristics shine through in her approach to design and teaching. Learning a new knitting skill like brioche takes practice, but it's easier when you feel like Lavanya is patiently holding your hand and guiding you through each new technique. Her patterns anticipate potentially difficult technical moments, and she always finds a way to make the design details more relaxing, intuitive, and fuss-free.

The Beginner's Brioche Cowl is the best place to start your first brioche project. Knitting brioche in the round is easier because you always knit the foreground color and you always purl the background color. These chunky accessories are super quick to knit, giving you a finished project that is equally practical and beautiful.

I was introduced to brioche knitting by the queen of brioche, Nancy Marchant, who shared her passion for this stitch during knit nights in Amsterdam. I finally took one of her workshops and I was immediately fascinated by the dimensional color and shaping possibilities of brioche knitting. Learning brioche felt like learning to knit all over again: it helps you understand the structure of knitted fabric and how to manipulate the stitches. Nancy is a brioche stitch magician who has dedicated years of her knitting life to spreading her love of brioche. I love how that inspiration has led me to meet other amazing knitters like Lavanya, who share the same passion for brioche and fascination for fiber.

There's something so magical and soothing about the quality of brioche knitting: it's such an elegant stitch with a divine drape and it produces a playful structure that is oh-so-soft and squishy. I am delighted to watch knitters from all around the world embrace this stitch. Knitters who fall in love with this technique are addicted and enchanted by its bouncy and reversible quality. I hope these tutorials and projects inspire you to unleash your creativity with brioche knitting. Once you catch the brioche bug, you will want to knit everything in brioche!

Stephen West

INTRODUCTION

In the winter of 2003 I asked my grandmother to teach me how to knit. I took to it quickly and began knitting my own sweaters and accessories almost immediately. I started teaching beginner knitting at local yarn shops and art spaces a few years later. I also did yarn bombing, exhibited in galleries, sold my hand-knit accessories at local boutiques, and worked part time at local yarn shops helping people with their own knit projects. It wasn't until the spring of 2013, after I had my first son, that I decided to try my hand at pattern writing in an effort to work from home.

In the winter of 2015 I came across a dress pattern by Stephen West that would change my life. I'd never seen the stitch before and knew as soon as I saw the fabric that I had to learn how to make it. I had no idea how much this magic little stitch would influence my creativity. The fabric was unique: it had a clear background and foreground, there were two colors and it was reversible. I made it my mission to learn how to make it and went on to knit my dream dress using the brioche technique. After finishing, I was hooked. I was inspired to design simple patterns, then more complex ones. I started teaching my first brioche classes at Conversational Threads Fiber Arts Studio in the summer of 2015. Before I knew it I was traveling around the country teaching knitters my favorite new stitch.

Here we are, almost a decade later, and not much has changed. I'm still in love with the stitch and still teaching dozens of people how to knit it every month. It's not a terribly hard stitch to learn but there are certain knitting rules that get broken or bent with brioche. Understanding the dynamics of how this fabric is made can really speed the learning process along. My hope with this book is to share with you what I've learned, through years of teaching both beginner and advanced knitters, about how to navigate the unique construction and terminology needed to knit this beautiful fabric successfully. You'll find clear written instructions with accompanying photographs, along with a collection of 15 patterns designed to follow you through your journey from mastering the beginning steps to more advanced skills. I also hope this book serves as a good reference for those who know how to work brioche but need a refresher, or are just looking for some inspiration.

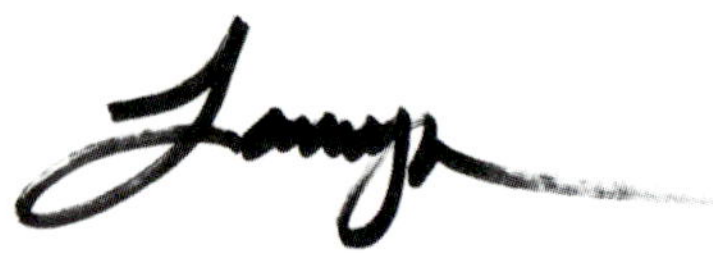

TOOLS AND MATERIALS

NEEDLES

Whether you are knitting brioche in the round or flat you will need circular or double-pointed needles. The reason for this is that it takes two passes to finish a row when working flat; you work half of your stitches on the first pass, then you will need to slide the stitches back to work the other half of the stitches on the second pass. The only way to achieve this is with circular or double-pointed needles. When working in the round you will still be following this two-pass rule—only you will not need to slide the stitches back because your yarn will be waiting for you at the end of each round.

YARN

Fiber type will greatly influence the fabric and drape in brioche after blocking. Plant-based fibers, superwash wools, pure wools, synthetics, alpaca, and silk all block out a little differently. Depending on what you are making this can have a pretty dramatic effect on your final product. I can't stress enough the importance of swatching and blocking to find your actual gauge (tension) when knitting a garment in brioche.

You can combine or swap fiber types in brioche patterns, but it's important to be aware that the fabric characteristics will change.

NOTIONS

Other handy tools to have are removable stitch markers. These markers are great for marking your right side and marking increases /decreases, and I find them especially useful for marking the beginning of your round or other important points in the pattern as they can help avoid yarn overs falling to the wrong side of the work at these transition points.

A crochet hook is also great to have for picking up dropped stitches.

BRIOCHE BASICS

CHOOSING COLORS

The first thing I'd like to talk about before anything else is color. Color placement will greatly affect the look of your final fabric, so here are my top tips and tricks for combining colors and choosing their placement. First let's talk about the stitches your foreground and background colors will align with in your patterns. Your brioche knit stitch (brk) color will be your foreground, it will be your pronounced and dominating color. Your brioche purl stitch (brp) color will be your background, it will be the complementary color to your foreground. The more contrast you have between your two colors, the more graphic and crisp your brioche ribbing will be.

Here's where color play comes in. On the right side my rule of thumb is if I have a dark color and a light color, dark is my background brp color and light is my foreground brk color. But what if we have a light and a bright color instead of light and dark? In this case I'd use my bright color as my background and light as my foreground—this makes for a bold and graphic fabric with crisp vertical lines. However, if I'm looking for a more subtle fabric, I'll want to reverse this order. Let's look at this visually, you can see in these photos how different the fabric looks with reversed color placements. A lot of brioche projects are reversible, but not all, so I recommend always making your color choices for your right side.

GETTING STARTED WITH BRIOCHE

Before we cast on, let's go over a few basics. Brioche is a very stretchy fabric that will require some give in the cast on. I personally use the knit on method for casting on but the longtail (continental) method works equally as well. Whatever cast on you choose you'll want to make sure to work it loosely, which may require casting on with a larger needle. Likewise for binding (casting) off. I often use a super-stretchy bind off because I find it matches the fabric very well, especially for shawls and openings where I will want more ease.

The terminology in brioche knitting will likely be new to you. Your three main stitches are the slip 1 stitch, yarn over (sl1yo), brioche knit (brk), and brioche purl (brp). The first stitch you will learn will be the sl1yo; this stitch is what makes it all happen. Each slipped stitch gets a yarn over—but here's the thing: yarn overs don't count as stitches in brioche. When you count your stitches the sl1yo counts as one stitch not two.

The brk and brp stitches are essentially a k2tog and p2tog—you will be knitting or purling the slipped stitch together with its yarn over. However, because yarn overs don't count as stitches in brioche, instead these stitches are called brk and brp. Your stitch count will only change in brioche when you are using specific increase or decrease stitches.

If you are a beginner, I recommend learning two-color brioche in the round first. Doing so gives you a lot of practice without having to remember to slide your stitches back or work the wrong side. The Beginner's Cowl is a fantastic first project. After you get a little practice in the round, working two-color brioche flat is pretty easy. I also personally think learning two-color brioche is a lot easier than learning one-color as a beginner. With two-color brioche you will find that the colors themselves are your guide. You are always slipping the opposite color you are working with and you are always brioche knitting or purling two colors together.

SAMPLE PATTERN OF BRIOCHE WORKED IN THE ROUND

Round 1 (Color A): *Sl1yo, k1; repeat from * to end of round.

Round 1 (Color B): *Brp, sl1yo; repeat from * to end of round.

PATTERN FOR TWO-COLOR BRIOCHE IN THE ROUND

When you read brioche patterns in the round you will see them written with Round 1 (Color A) for the first pass, followed by Round 1 (Color B) for the second pass. You don't move on to Round 2 until both passes are completed. Brioche is a ribbing in which every other stitch is slipped. When working in the round, you will be brioche knitting half of the stitches in one color on the first pass, and brioche purling the other half of the stitches in another color on the second pass. Remember there is no need to twist your yarns at the beginning of your round when switching colors. This is a seamless fabric and the yarn will be right where it needs to be at the end of each completed round.

SAMPLE PATTERN OF BRIOCHE WORKED FLAT

Row 1 (Color A RS): K1, brk, *sl1yo, brk; repeat from * to last st, k1.

Row 1 (Color B RS): P1, sl1yo, *brp, sl1yo; repeat from * to last st, p1.

Row 2 (Color A WS): P1, brp, *sl1yo, brp; repeat from * to last st, p1.

Row 2 (Color B WS): K1, sl1yo, *brk, sl1yo; repeat from * to last st, k1.

PATTERN FOR TWO-COLOR BRIOCHE FLAT

When knitting two-color brioche flat you will have two right-side passes and two wrong-side passes. As noted earlier you will still need circular or double-pointed needles though: on your first right-side pass you will be brioche knitting half of the stitches in the first color, then you will need to slide the stitches back to work a right-side brioche purl pass in another color on the other half of the stitches. After you've completed both passes on the right side, you'll turn your work and complete two wrong-side passes. It's important to note that your right-side brk color will be your brp color on the wrong side and your right-side brp color will be your brk color on the wrong side.

MEASURING GAUGE / TENSION

When measuring gauge, after blocking you will lay your measuring tape across the work. It's important not to stretch the fabric but to measure it as it lays. I like to start counting from a brk stitch, which will resemble a stockinette stitch on the right side. It's also easiest to count your row gauge from your brk stitch. Here you can see I am getting 4 stitches to 2.5cm (1in).

BRIOCHE STITCHES

Every brioche pattern begins with casting on the required number of stitches, and then completing a set up row for brioche in either knit or purl as follows.

SET UP KNITWISE

This set up row will introduce your second color and get you established for your brioche stitches. After completing this row, you will proceed with a brioche purl row, then work your full pattern repetition.

1. With Color A yarn in front, slip one Color B stitch purlwise.
2. Bring the Color A yarn over the needle to create a yarn over; this also brings your yarn to the back into the knitting position.
3. Knit the next Color B stitch.
4. Repeat these three steps to the end of the round or row.

SET UP PURLWISE

This set up row will introduce your second color and get you established for your brioche stitches. After completing this row you will proceed with a brioche knit row, then work your full pattern repetition.

1. Using Color A yarn, purl one Color B stitch.
2. With Color A yarn in front, slip one Color B stitch purlwise.
3. Bring the Color A yarn all the way around the right-hand needle back into purling position to create a yarn over.
4. Repeat these three steps to the end of the round or row.

BRIOCHE KNIT

This sequence involves slipping one stitch purlwise, making a yarn over, then working a brioche knit, which is abbreviated in the patterns as "sl1yo, brk".

1. With the Color A yarn in front, slip one Color B stitch purlwise.
2. Bring the Color A yarn over the right-hand needle towards the back, creating a yarn over.
3. To brioche knit (brk), you will be knitting together the slipped stitch and the yarn over from the previous row. This will look like a Color A stitch with a Color B yarn over on top of it, so enter both as if to knit. If you've ever worked a k2tog, this is pretty much the same thing, only it's not a decrease.
4. The finished stitch. It's important to always remember to bring your yarn to the front before you slip and to yarn over after you slip.

TIP

As you knit this repetition you will find that it becomes one movement: as you bring the yarn to the back over the needle to brioche knit, you create the yarn over for your slipped stitch.

BRIOCHE PURL

This sequence involves working a brioche purl stitch, slipping one stitch purlwise, then working a yarn over, which is abbreviated in the patterns as "brp, sl1yo".

1. To brioche purl (brp), you will be purling together the slipped stitch and yarn over from the previous row. This will look like a Color B stitch with a Color A yarn over on top of it; enter both as if to purl. If you've ever done a p2tog, this is pretty much the same thing only it's not a decrease.
2. Because we have purled a stitch, the Color B yarn is already in front, ready to slip the next stitch purlwise.
3. Slip the Color A stitch purlwise.
4. Bring the Color B yarn all the way around the right-hand needle until it is back in the purling position. I like to call this the "Big Yarn Over" when I'm teaching classes because it requires a full wrap around the needle. This makes the finished stitch. It's important to always remember to yarn over after you slip your stitch.

> **TIP**
>
> *In two-color brioche you will always be slipping the stitch in the opposite color to what you are working with and you will always be brioche knitting or purling together one strand of each color.*

INCREASES

Now that we've mastered the basics let's move on to the stitches that add to the magic. I'll be showing you how to do two different increases in this section. The brkyobrk and the brpyobrp are both two-stitch increases and are by far the most commonly used in brioche patterns.

TWO-STITCH INCREASE (KNIT)

To increase in knit you work a brioche knit stitch, yarn over, brioche knit stitch, which is abbreviated in the patterns as "brkyobrk".

1. Using Color A, enter the stitch as if to brioche knit it, pull your yarn all the way through but leave the stitch on the needle.
2. Take Color A yarn over on the right-hand needle.
3. Using Color A, go into the brioche stitch and knit once more, then let the stitch off the left-hand needle after completing. This will look like three Color A stitches coming out of one brioche knit stitch on your right-hand needle
4. When you come to your increase on a brioche purl pass, the Color B yarn should be in the front. Slip the first leg of the increase onto the right-hand needle and yarn over.
5. Using Color B, purl the second leg of the stitch.
6. Then slip the last leg of the stitch purlwise and yarn over with Color B. You've now successfully increased your stitch count by two and are back in pattern.

CONTINENTAL

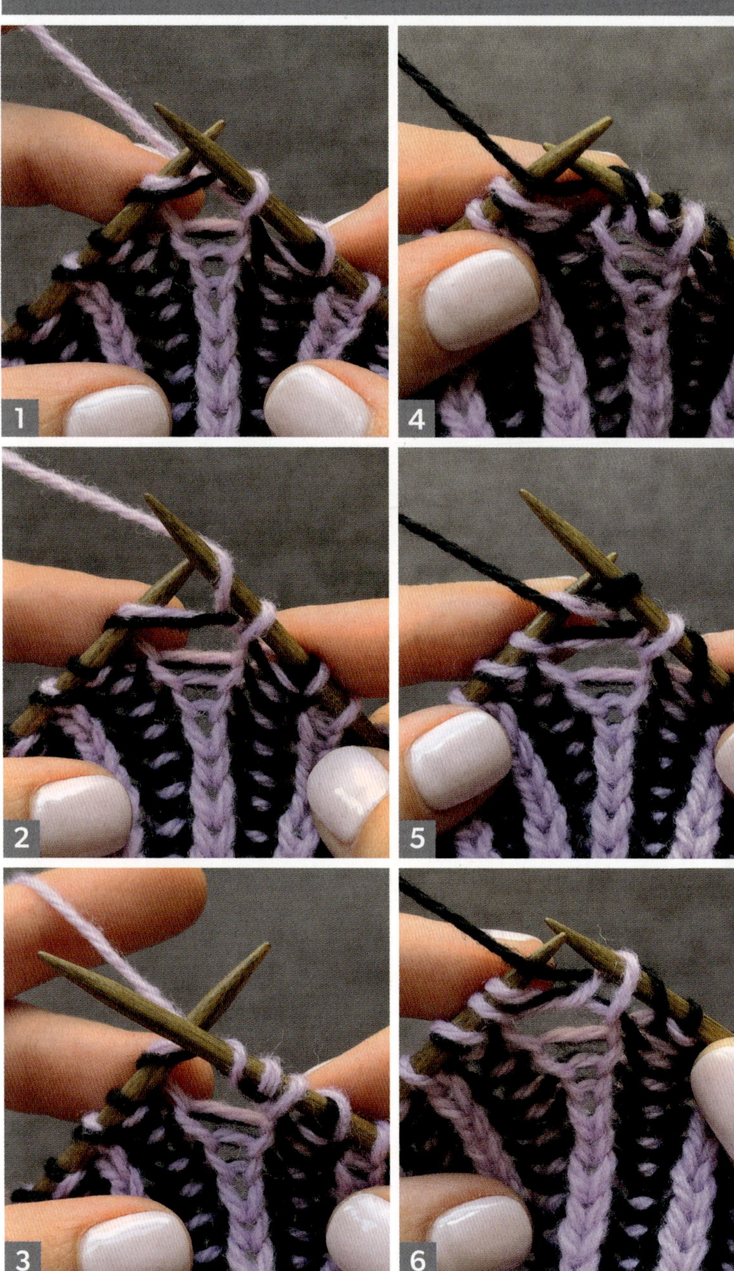

TIPS

Note that because brioche is a ribbing stitch, you will need to increase by two—or a multiple of two—stitches at a time in order to stay in pattern.

For other types of increases used in some of the patterns, see the General Techniques section.

ENGLISH

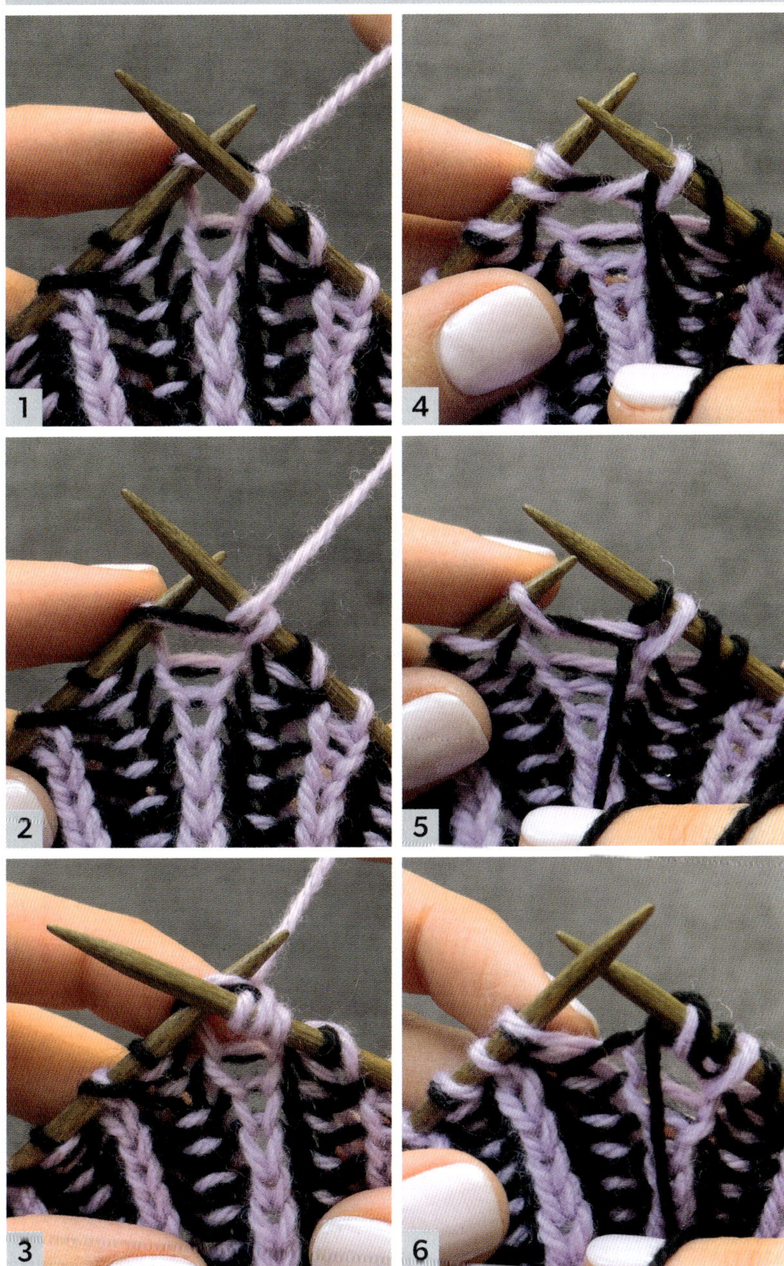

TIP

You can easily turn this two-stitch increase into a four-stitch increase instead if your pattern should call for it, by working Step 1, then repeating Steps 2 and 3 twice without letting the stitch off the left hand needle on the first repetition. Then work Step 4, and finally repeat Steps 5 and 6 twice.

CONTINENTAL

TWO-STITCH INCREASE (PURL)

To increase in purl you work a brioche purl stitch, yarn over, brioche purl stitch, which is abbreviated in the patterns as "brpyobrp".

1. Using Color B, enter the stitch as if to brioche purl it, then pull your yarn all the way through but leave the stitch on the needle.
2. Take Color B yarn over on the right-hand needle.
3. Using Color B, go into the brioche stitch and purl once more, then let the stitch off the left-hand needle after completing.
4. When you come to your increase on a brioche knit pass, the Color A yarn should be in the front. Slip the first leg of the increase onto the right-hand needle and yarn over.
5. Using Color A, knit the second leg of the stitch.
6. Then slip the last leg of the stitch purlwise and yarn over with Color A. You've now successfully increased your stitch count by two and are back in pattern.

TIP

You can easily turn this two-stitch increase into a four-stitch increase instead if your pattern should call for it, by working Step 1, then repeating Steps 2 and 3 twice without letting the stitch off the left hand needle on the first repetition. Then work Step 4, and finally repeat Steps 5 and 6 twice.

ENGLISH

TIPS

Remember that because brioche is a ribbing stitch, you will have to increase by two—or a multiple of two—stitches at a time in order to stay in pattern.

For other types of increases used in some of the patterns, see the General Techniques section.

DECREASES

There are many different decrease techniques in brioche but these are the two that get used more than any others. Just as explained in the Increase section, you will need to decrease by two stitches in order to stay in pattern. In order to decrease by two you will need to use three stitches in your decrease. The brLsl is your left slanting decrease and the brRsl is your right slanting decrease.

TWO-STITCH DECREASE (LEFT LEANING)

This is a two-stitch decrease that slants to the left, involving three stitches, which is abbreviated in the patterns as "brLsl".

1. Using Color A, slip the first brk stitch, including its yarn over, knitwise.
2. Brk the following two stitches together; remember this will look like three stitches because it includes the yarn over.
3. Pass the slipped brk stitch, including its yarn over, over the last worked stitch.
4. The finished stitch. You've now successfully decreased your stitch count by two and are back in pattern.

TWO-STITCH DECREASE (RIGHT LEANING)

This is a two-stitch decrease that slants to the right, involving three stitches, which is abbreviated in the patterns as "brRsl".

1. Using Color A, slip the first brk stitch, including its yarn over, knitwise.
2. Knit the next stitch. Note that it is a single Color B purl stitch that you are knitting.
3. Pass the slipped stitch, including its yarn over, over the last worked stitch.
4. Slip this stitch back to the left-hand needle
5. Pass the following brk stitch over, including its yarn over.
6. Slip the stitch back to the right-hand needle.
7. The finished stitch. You've now successfully decreased your stitch count by two and are back in pattern.

CONTINENTAL

TIP

Many patterns use these decreases as well as the stitche from the Increases section. The are used for shaping but also to create beautiful motifs. You can think of intricate brioche patterns like lace; the pattern is created by a repetition of increases and decreases.

ENGLISH

BRIOCHE STITCH VARIATIONS

Let's look at a few interesting stitch variations and go over how to work them with what you've learned so far. You will find these techniques featured in some of the patterns later on in the book.

SYNCOPATION

Syncopated brioche is a super fun way to add texture and break up the stripes in brioche. You will follow a standard brioche repeat to a certain point and then you will have a row where you flip your stitches so that your brioche purl stitches are now on top of your brioche knit stitches and vice versa.

You repeat this process of switching the stitches throughout the pattern. It's important to note that the first pass of syncopated brioche will be all one color until you reintroduce the second color in its new stitch orientation. You can see this technique in the Residents Shawl.

SAMPLE PATTERN OF SYNCOPATION WORKED IN THE ROUND

Round 1 (Color A): *Sl1yo, brp; repeat from * to end of round.

Round 1 (Color B): *Brk, sl1yo; repeat from * to end of round.

Round 2 (Color B): *Sl1yo, brk; repeat from * to end of round.

Round 2 (Color A): *Brp, sl1yo; repeat from * to end of round.

SAMPLE PATTERN OF SYNCOPATION WORKED FLAT

Row 2 (RS Color A): K2, *brk, sl1yo; repeat from * to last 3 sts, brk, k2.

Row 2 (RS Color B): P2, *sl1yo, brp; repeat from * to last 3 sts, sl1yo, p2.

Row 3 (WS Color B): P2 *brk, sl1yo; repeat from * to last 3 sts, brk, p2.

Row 3 (WS Color A): K2, *sl1yo, brp; repeat from * to last 3 sts, slyo, k2.

TIP

Life lines—strands of contrast waste yarn the same weight as your main yarn, that are pulled through the stitches at set points—are a great tool when working on more complex patterns, or as beginners when the likelihood of making mistakes is a lot higher.

ONE-COLOR BRIOCHE

After you've worked two- color brioche, one-color brioche is easy. Since you are only working in one color, when you transition from your brioche purl round back to your brioche knit round you will have a sl1yo before and after the marker, which will feel counterintuitive but is correct.

When knitting one-color brioche flat there is only one right side and one wrong side pass; since there is no second color, there is no need to slide the stitches back. You will also generally only work brk/sl1yo when knitting one-color brioche flat. You can see this stitch in the One-color Brioche Hat.

SAMPLE PATTERN OF ONE-COLOR BRIOCHE WORKED IN THE ROUND

Round 1: *Sl1yo, brk; repeat from * to end of round.

Round 2: *Brp, sl1yo; repeat from * to end of round.

Round 3: *Sl1yo, brk; repeat from * to end of round.

Round 4: *Brp, sl1yo; repeat from * to end of round.

SAMPLE PATTERN OF ONE-COLOR BRIOCHE WORKED FLAT

Row 1: K1, *brk, sl1yo; repeat from * to last 2 sts, brk, k1.

Row 2: K1, *sl1yo, brk; repeat from * to last 2 sts, sl1yo, k1.

BRIOCHE AND GARTER

Garter stitch matches gauge (tension) with brioche wonderfully so it's a great stitch to mix in. I love the combination of textures and directions garter brings into the fabric. In order to knit two-color garter stitch in the round you are going to have to knit the first pass in one color and purl the second pass in the other color.

If you are working two-color garter stitch flat, you'll knit the first pass, then slide your stitches up and purl your second pass. When you turn to work the wrong side you will purl the first pass and knit the second pass in order to maintain the garter stitch pattern. You can see these stitches combined in the Split Bandana Cowl.

SAMPLE PATTERN OF BRIOCHE AND GARTER WORKED IN THE ROUND

Round 3 (Color A): K to marker, SM, brk, *sl1yo, brk; repeat from * to end of round.

Round 3 (Color B): P to marker, SM, sl1yo, *brp, sl1yo; repeat from * to end of round.

SAMPLE PATTERN OF BRIOCHE AND GARTER WORKED FLAT

Row 4 (RS Color A): K8, *[brk, sl1yo] 3 times, brk, k8.

Row 4 (RS Color B): P8, *[sl1yo, brp] 3 times, sl1yo, p8.

Row 5 (WS Color A): P8, *[brp, sl1yo] 3 times, brp, p8.

Row 5 (WS Color B): K8, *[sl1yo, brk] 3 times, sl1yo, k8.

TROUBLESHOOTING

Well the unimaginable has happened—actually it's completely imaginable in brioche—you've made a mistake! They happen to the best of us. The truth is learning brioche isn't too hard but not knowing what to do when things go wrong is where people get stuck and oftentimes give up. Here are a few of the most common and helpful troubleshooting tips to get you through the inevitable.

DROPPED STITCHES / DROPPING A STITCH TO FIX IT

So you've dropped a stitch, or maybe you made a mistake and you need to drop a stitch to fix it. Whatever the case it's not as scary as it looks. If you've ever laddered up a dropped stockinette (stocking) stitch you can do this, too! Let me show you how. It's always easier to ladder up on a brioche knit stitch so be sure to turn and work your wrong side if you've dropped a brioche purl. I recommend doing this with a crochet hook because it's easier to do but you can do it with a needle if necessary. If you look closely at the stitch you will see it has a strand of each color linked together, here's how to ladder these two threads back up.

1. Grab your live stitch, this looks just like a live stockinette stitch, and place it on the crochet hook. Note that this stitch has just one strand of contrast color yarn below.
2. Go behind the strands of contrast color yarn and hook your next presenting main color yarn, pull this through brioche knit stitch. Note that this stitch also has just one strand of contrast yarn below.
3. Repeat this process until you've laddered all the way up to where you need to be.
4. To finish, place the dropped stitch back on the needle.

1

2

3

4

DROPPED YARN OVERS PURL AND KNIT STITCH

One of the most common mistakes I see when I'm teaching is the missing yarn over. Sometimes we forget to do a yarn over when we slip and that yarn falls to the back or front of the work. This is a super easy mistake to fix but causes chaos pretty quickly if you don't catch it. Many times when we don't notice that the yarn over is missing we end up working two actual stitches together because we are looking for both colors. When this happens we are not only decreasing our stitch count but also removing a color all together. Here's how to recover your missing yarn over so this doesn't happen.

RS knit stitch dropped yarn over in the front:

1. With the right-hand needle pick up the dropped yarn over from below and then insert the needle into the knit stitch.
2. Slip both strands onto the right-hand needle as if to knit.
3. Using the left-hand needle, slip the recovered yarn over and stitch back onto the left-hand needle. It's now ready to brioche knit.

RS knit stitch dropped yarn over in the back:

1. With the left-hand needle, identify the top bar of color in the back as pictured.
2. Pick up the yarn over from the back and place it back on the left-hand needle. It's now ready to brioche knit.

1

2

3

TIP

If your dropped yarn over is in the back and you are unsure of which strand of yarn to grab, look for the strand that is connected to the following stitch on the needle; that will be your dropped yarn over.

1

2

RS purl stitch dropped yarn over in the front:

1. With the right-hand needle, pick up the dropped yarn over from below and then insert the needle into the purl stitch.
2. Slip both strands onto the right-hand needle as if to knit.
3. Using the left-hand needle, slip the recovered yarn over and stitch back to the left-hand needle. It's now ready to brioche purl.

TIP

If you are unsure which strand is your yarn over, to identify it look for the yarn over that is looser and sits above the stitch that it has dropped into.

RS purl stitch dropped yarn over in the back:

1. With the left-hand needle, pick up the yarn over from the back.
2. Place it back on the left-hand needle. It's now ready to brioche purl.

WEAVING IN

Weaving in ends in brioche isn't always self explanatory. My favorite way to do it can be worked with both your Color A and Color B yarn.

1. With WS facing, using a darning needle, bring the yarn up through the left- or right-slanting side of your brp stitch; I usually draw the yarn through about four to seven rows of stitches.
2. Bring the yarn all the way through and let it hang. I advise blocking first, then cutting your ends!

TINKING / UNRAVELLING

The sad truth is it happens; sometimes we just have to rip back a little. If you've made a mistake, picked up the wrong color, or missed a crucial part of a pattern repeat, repeat these three steps to unknit as many stitches as you need to.

Tinking a brioche knit row

1. Using the left-hand needle, enter the brioche knit stitch from below making sure to secure both strands of yarn.
2. Unravel the working yarn from the stitch.
3. Drop the yarn over and slip the purl stitch back onto the left-hand needle, do not unravel it.

TIP

It's important to note that you are only undoing one color at a time, so if you are ripping back on a brioche knit row you will only be unraveling a brioche knit stitch and slipping the purl stitch back.

Tinking a brioche purl row

1. Using the left-hand needle, enter the brioche purl stitch from below, making sure to secure both strands of yarn.
2. Unravel the working yarn from the stitch.
3. Drop the yarn over and slip the purl stitch back to the left-hand needle, do not unravel it.

TIP

Again remember that you are only undoing one color at a time, so if you are ripping back on a brioche purl row you will only be unraveling a brioche purl stitch and slipping the knit stitch back.

PROJECTS

BEGINNER'S BRIOCHE COWL

This one is designed especially for beginners; if you are looking for a starting pattern this is it! The bulky yarn and simple repetition in this cowl makes it the perfect first project.

MATERIALS

- Color A: 80yd (73m) bulky (chunky) weight yarn *(Sample: Malabrigo Yarns, Chunky in Rosalinda)*
- Color B: 95yd (87m) bulky (chunky) weight yarn *(Sample: Malabrigo Yarns, Chunky in Whole Grain)*
- US 11 (8mm), 16in (40cm) circular needles
- 1 stitch marker

GAUGE (TENSION)

10 sts x 12 rows = 4in (10cm) in two-color brioche stitch on US 11 (8mm) needles, or size needed to obtain gauge.

MEASUREMENTS

23in (58.5cm) around x 14in (35.5cm) tall

NOTE

Remember to begin with the yarn in front before working the slipped stitch at the beginning of Rounds 2 and 3 in Color A.

ABBREVIATIONS

brk	Brioche knit: knit slipped stitch together with its yarn over
brp	Brioche purl: purl slipped stitch together with its yarn over
CO	Cast on
k	Knit stitch
p	Purl stitch
PM	Place marker
sl1yo	With yarn in front, slip 1 stitch purlwise, yarn over
wyif	With yarn in front

INSTRUCTIONS

Using US 11 (8mm) needles and Color B, CO 58 sts.

Being careful not to twist sts, PM and join in the round.

Round 1: *P1, k1; repeat from * to end of round.

Round 2 (Color A): *Sl1yo, k1; repeat from * to end of round (leave Color B in back).

Round 2 (Color B): *Brp, sl1yo; repeat from * to end of round (leave Color A in front).

Round 3 (Color A): *Sl1yo, brk; repeat from * to end of round (leave Color B in back).

Round 3 (Color B): *Brp, sl1yo; repeat from * to end of round (leave Color A in front).

Repeat Round 3 another 38 times or until desired length is reached.

Break Color A.

Round 4 (Color B): *P1, brk; repeat from * to end of round.

Bind (cast) off loosely, cut yarn and draw through remaining st.

Weave in ends and wet block to set sts.

FIRST BRIOCHE HAT

This stylish slouch hat is a simple unisex design. Knit in simple two-color brioche, the hat utilizes brioche decreasing in the crown shaping, making it a great step forward into the next level of skills while remaining very beginner friendly. For a single color version see the One-color Brioche Hat.

MATERIALS

- Color A: 110yd (101m) DK weight yarn *(Sample: West Wool, Tandem in Birch Tree)*
- Color B: 80yd (73m) DK weight yarn *(Sample: West Wool, Tandem in Copenhagen)*
- US 4 (3.5mm), 16in (40cm) circular needles
- US 4 (3.5mm) double-pointed needles (DPNs)
- 1 stitch marker

GAUGE (TENSION)

23 sts x 21 rows = 4in (10cm) in two-color brioche stitch on US 4 (3.5mm) needles, or size needed to obtain gauge.

MEASUREMENTS

9 x 19in (23 x 48cm)

The hat is super stretchy, will fit a 22–25in (56–63.5cm) head comfortably.

ABBREVIATIONS

brk	Brioche knit: knit slipped stitch together with its yarn over
brLsl	A 2-stitch decrease that slants to the left, involving 3 stitches: slip the first stitch knitwise, brk the following 2 stitches together, pass the slipped stitch over
brp	Brioche purl: purl slipped stitch together with its yarn over
CO	Cast on
k	Knit stitch
k2tog	Knit 2 stitches together
p	Purl stitch
PM	Place marker
sl1yo	With yarn in front, slip 1 stitch purlwise, yarn over

INSTRUCTIONS

Using US 4 (3.5mm) circular needles and Color A, CO 112 sts.

Being careful not to twist sts, PM and join in the round.

Rounds 1 to 18: *P1, k1; repeat from * to end of round.

Round 19 (Color B): *P1, sl1yo; repeat from * to end of round.

Round 20 (Color A): *Sl1yo, brk; repeat from * to end of round.

Round 20 (Color B): *Brp, sl1yo; repeat from * to end of round.

Repeat Round 20 until work measures 7½in (19cm) from cast-on edge.

BEGIN DECREASE SHAPING:

(Switching to DPNs when necessary)

Round 21 (Color A): *Sl1yo, brLsl, [sl1yo, brk] 5 times; repeat from * to end of round. (96 sts)

Round 21 (Color B): *Brp, sl1yo; repeat from * to end of round.

Round 22 (Color A): *Sl1yo, brk; repeat from * to end of round.

Round 22 (Color B): *Brp, sl1yo; repeat from * to end of round.

Round 23 (Color A): *Sl1yo, brLsl, [sl1yo, brk] 4 times; repeat from * to end of round. (80 sts)

Round 23 (Color B): *Brp, sl1yo; repeat from * to end of round.

Round 24 (Color A): *Sl1yo, brk; repeat from * to end of round.

Round 24 (Color B): *Brp, sl1yo; repeat from * to end of round.

Round 25 (Color A): *Sl1yo, brLsl, [sl1yo, brk] 3 times; repeat from * to end of round. (64 sts)

Round 25 (Color B): *Brp, sl1yo; repeat from * to end of round.

Round 26 (Color A): *Sl1yo, brk; repeat from * to end of round.

Round 26 (Color B): *Brp, sl1yo; repeat from * to end of round.

Round 27 (Color A): *Sl1yo, brLsl, [sl1yo, brk] twice; repeat from * to end of round. (48 sts)

Round 27 (Color B): *Brp, sl1yo; repeat from * to end of round.

Round 28 (Color A): *Sl1yo, brk; repeat from * to end of round.

Round 28 (Color B): *Brp, sl1yo; repeat from * to end of round.

Round 29 (Color A): *Sl1yo, brLsl, sl1yo, brk; repeat from * to end of round. (32 sts)

Round 29 (Color B): *Brp, sl1yo; repeat from * to end of round.

Round 30 (Color A): *Sl1yo, brk; repeat from * to end of round.

Round 30 (Color B): *Brp, sl1yo; repeat from * to end of round.

Round 31 (Color A): *Sl1yo, brLsl; repeat from * to end of round. (16 sts)

Round 31 (Color B): *Brp, sl1yo; repeat from * to end of round, break color B.

Round 32 (Color A): *K1, brk; repeat from * to end of round.

Round 33 (Color A): *K2tog; repeat from * to end of round. (8 sts)

Cut tail, draw through remaining sts to fasten off.

Weave in ends and wet block to set sts.

BEGINNER'S BRIOCHE SCARF

This is the perfect pattern for beginners who want to learn how to knit two-color brioche flat. The length is customizable and the super bulky (chunky) yarn knits up fast!

MATERIALS

- Color A: 180yd (165m) super bulky (super chunky) weight yarn
  (*Sample: Malabrigo Yarns, Rasta in Frank Ochre*)
- Color B: 180yd (165m) of super bulky (super chunky) weight yarn
  (*Sample: Malabrigo Yarns, Rasta in Plomo*)
- US 13 (9mm) 24in (60cm) circular needles
- Crochet hook (to attach fringe, optional)

GAUGE (TENSION)

9 sts x 16 rows = 4in (10cm) in two-color brioche stitch on US 13 (9mm) needles, or size needed to obtain gauge.

MEASUREMENTS

6in (15cm) wide x 106in (269cm) long

NOTE

When knitting two-color brioche flat remember that it takes two passes to equal a row. On your RS row you will work the first pass [brk] in Color A, then slide the stitches back to work the second pass [brp] in Color B, completing one RS row. You'll know you have finished both passes of a row when the A/B yarns are on the right needle ready to be turned for the WS row. You'll repeat this for the WS row with stitches reversed, Color A [brp] and Color B [brk], turning to work RS after both passes are complete.

ABBREVIATIONS

brk	Brioche knit: knit slipped stitch together with its yarn over
brp	Brioche purl: purl slipped stitch together with its yarn over
CO	Cast on
k	Knit stitch
p	Purl stitch
sl1yo	With yarn in front, slip 1 stitch purlwise, yarn over
sl1	Slip 1 stitch purlwise

INSTRUCTIONS

Using US 13 (9mm) needles and Color B, CO 13 sts.

Row 1 (RS Color B): K to end of row.

Row 2 (WS Color A): P1, *p1, sl1yo; repeat from * to last 2 sts, p2.

Row 2 (WS Color B): K1, *sl1yo, brk; repeat from * to last 2 sts, sl1yo, k1, turn to work RS.

Row 3 (RS Color A): K1, *brk, sl1yo; repeat from * to last 2 sts, brk, k1.

Row 3 (RS Color B): P1, *sl1yo, brp; repeat from * to last 2 sts, sl1yo, p1, turn to work WS.

Row 4 (WS Color A): P1, *brp, sl1yo; repeat from * to last 2 sts, brp, p1.

Row 4 (WS Color B): K1, *sl1yo, brk; repeat from * to last 2 sts, sl1yo, k1, turn to work RS.

Repeat Rows 3 and 4 to desired length (sample is 90in/228.5cm) blocked to 106in/269cm using 2 balls of each color).

Break Color A.

Row 5 (Color B): K1, *brk, k1; repeat from * to end of row.

Bind (cast) off loosely, cut tail and draw through remaining st.

Weave in ends and wet block to set sts.

OPTIONAL FRINGE

Cut 10in (25cm) lengths of remaining Color A yarn. Using four strands of yarn per tassel, fold in half and pull top of folded loop through bottom edge of a Color A brk st using a crochet hook. Take all ends through loop to make a lark's head knot and pull to tighten tassel in place. Repeat 5 more times in remaining edge brk sts. Repeat for other side.

ADVANCING LINES SCARF

IIIIIIIIIIIIIII

I designed this scarf to teach people how to use brioche increases and decreases. It's a simple repeat that makes a great unisex design. The length of the scarf is completely customizable and the worsted (aran) weight yarn knits up fast!

MATERIALS

- Color A: 200yd (183m) worsted (aran) weight yarn
  (Sample: Farmers Daughter Fibers, Pishkun in Mountain Man)
- Color B: 200yd (183m) worsted (aran) weight yarn
  (Sample: Farmers Daughter Fibers, Pishkun in The Den)
- US 7 (4.5mm), 16in (40cm) circular needles

GAUGE (TENSION)

15 sts x 19 rows = 4in (10cm) in stitch pattern on US 7 (4.5mm) needles or size needed to obtain gauge.

MEASUREMENTS

5½ x 93in (14 x 236cm)

NOTE

When knitting two-color brioche flat remember that it takes two passes to equal a row. On your RS row you will work the first pass [brk] in Color A, then slide the stitches back to work the second pass [brp] in Color B, completing one RS row. You'll know you have finished both passes of a row when the A/B yarns are on the right needle ready to be turned for the WS row. You'll repeat this for the WS row with stitches reversed, Color A [brp] and Color B [brk], turning to work RS after both passes are complete.

ABBREVIATIONS

brk	Brioche knit: knit slipped stitch together with its yarn over
brkyobrk	A 2-stitch increase in brioche knit: brioche knit, yarn over, brioche knit into the same stitch
brLsl	A 2-stitch decrease that slants to the left, involving three stitches: slip the first stitch knitwise, brk the following two stitches together, pass the slipped stitch over
brRsl	A 2-stitch decrease that slants to the right, involving three stitches: slip the first stitch knitwise, knit the next stitch, pass the slipped stitch over, place stitch on left hand needle and pass the following stitch over. Place stitch back on right hand needle
brp	Brioche purl: purl slipped stitch together with its yarn over
CO	Cast on
k	Knit stitch
p	Purl stitch
sl1yo	With yarn in front, slip 1 stitch purlwise, yarn over

INSTRUCTIONS

Using US 7 (4.5mm) needles and Color B, CO 21 sts.

Rows 1 and 2: K to end of row.

Row 3 (RS Color A): K2, *sl1yo, k1; repeat from * to last st, k1.

Row 3 (RS Color B): P1, sl1yo, *brp, sl1yo; repeat from * to last st, p1.

Row 4 (WS Color A): P1, brp, *sl1yo, brp; repeat from * to last st, p1.

Row 4 (WS Color B): K1, sl1yo, *brk, sl1yo; repeat from * to last st, k1.

Row 5 (RS Color A): K1, brk, *sl1yo, brk; repeat from * to last st, k1.

Row 5 (RS Color B): P1, sl1yo, *brp, sl1yo; repeat from * to last st, p1.

Row 6 (WS Color A): P1, brp, *sl1yo, brp; repeat from * to last st, p1.

Row 6 (WS Color B): K1, sl1yo, *brk, sl1yo; repeat from * to last st, k1.

Row 7 (RS Color A): K1, [brk, sl1yo] 4 times, brkyobrk, sl1yo, brkyobrk, [sl1yo, brk] 4 times, k1. (25 sts)

Row 7 (RS Color B): P1, [sl1yo, brp] 4 times, sl1yo, p1, sl1yo, brp, sl1yo, p1, sl1yo, [brp, sl1yo] 4 times, p1.

Row 8 (WS Color A): P1, brp, *sl1yo, brp; repeat from * to last st, p1.

Row 8 (WS Color B): K1, sl1yo, *brk, sl1yo; repeat from * to last st, k1.

Row 9 (RS Color A): K1, [brk, sl1yo] twice, brLsl, [sl1yo, brk] 4 times, sl1yo, brRsl, [sl1yo, brk] twice, k1. (21 sts)

Row 9 (RS Color B): P1, sl1yo, *brp, sl1yo; repeat from * to last st, p1.

Row 10 (WS Color A): P1, brp, *sl1yo, brp; repeat from * to last st, p1.

Row 10 (WS Color B): K1, sl1yo, *brk, sl1yo; repeat from * to last st, k1.

Repeat Rows 5 to 10 to desired length.

Break Color A.

Row 11 (Color B RS): K1, *brk, k1; repeat from * to end of row.

Row 12 (Color B WS): K all sts.

Bind (cast) off loosely.

Weave in ends and wet block to set sts.

SPLIT BANDANA COWL

This stylish cowl is worked in a combination of two-color brioche stitch and garter stitch. The pattern is worked both in the round and flat, with tapered shaping in the back so it fits nicely around the neck and under a jacket.

MATERIALS

- Color A: 120yd (110m) DK weight yarn *(Sample: West Wool, Tandem in Tangerine)*
- Color B: 100yd (92m) DK weight yarn *(Sample: West Wool, Tandem in Sherbert)*
- US 5 (3.75mm), 16in (40cm) circular needles
- 1 stitch marker

GAUGE (TENSION)

15 sts x 22 rows = 4in (10cm) in two-color brioche stitch on US 5 (3.75mm) needles, or size needed to obtain gauge.

MEASUREMENTS

22in (56cm) around, 14in (35.5cm) from cast on to point.

NOTE

When knitting brioche flat, remember it takes two passes to equal a row. To be more specific, on a RS row you will work the first pass [brk] in Color B, then slide the stitches up to work the second pass [brp] in Color A, completing one RS row. You'll know you have finished both passes of a row when the A/B yarns are on the right needle ready to be turned for the WS row. You'll repeat this for the WS row with stitches reversed, Color A [brp] and Color B [brk], turning to work RS after both passes are complete.

ABBREVIATIONS

brk	Brioche knit: knit slipped stitch together with its yarn over
brp	Brioche purl: purl slipped stitch together with its yarn over
brRsl	A 2-stitch decrease that slants to the right, involving three stitches: slip the first stitch knitwise, knit the next stitch, pass the slipped stitch over, place stitch on left hand needle and pass the following stitch over. Place stitch back on right hand needle
CO	Cast on using the knit on method
k	Knit stitch
k2tog	Knit 2 stitches together
k3tog	Knit 3 stitches together
p	Purl stitch
PM / SM	Place marker / slide marker
psso	Pass slipped stitch over
sl1	Slip 1 stitch purlwise
sl1yo	With yarn in front, slip 1 stitch purlwise, yarn over
wyib / wyif	With yarn in back / with yarn in front

INSTRUCTIONS

Using US 5 (3.75mm) needles and Color A, CO 88 sts.

Being careful not to twist sts, PM and join in the round

Round 1: P43, PM, k1, *p1, k1; repeat from * to end of round.

Round 2 (Color B): K to marker, SM, k1, *sl1yo, k1; repeat from * to end of round

Round 2 (Color A): P to marker, SM, sl1yo, *brp, sl1yo; repeat from * to end of round.

Round 3 (Color B): K to marker, SM, brk, *sl1yo, brk; repeat from * to end of round.

Round 3 (Color A): P to marker, SM, sl1yo, *brp, sl1yo; repeat from * to end of round.

Work Round 3 another 34 times.

> *NOTE: You should be able to count 36 knit column rows in Color B.*

Round 38 (Color B): K to marker, SM, brk, *sl1yo, brk; repeat from * to end of round.

Round 38 (Color A): P to marker, SM, sl1yo, *brp, sl1yo; repeat from * to last 2 sts, brp, k1, pass last worked brp over. (87 sts)

Remove marker, turn to work wrong side. You will now be working flat.

Row 39 (WS Color B): Wyif sl1, *brp, sl1yo; repeat from * to marker, SM, p to end of round.

Row 39 (WS Color A): K1, sl1yo, *brk, sl1yo; repeat from * to marker, SM, k to end of round.

Row 40 (RS Color B): Wyib sl1, k3tog, k to marker, SM, *brk, sl1yo; repeat from * to last 4 sts, brRsl, wyib sl1. (83 sts)

Row 40 (RS Color A): K1, p to marker, SM, sl1yo, *brp, sl1yo; repeat from * to last st, k1.

Row 41 (WS Color B): Wyif sl1, *brp, sl1yo; repeat from * to marker, SM, p to end of round.

Row 41 (WS Color A): K1, sl1yo, *brk, sl1yo; repeat from * to marker, SM, k to end of round.

Work Rows 40 and 41 another 19 times. (7 sts)

Row 80 (RS Color B): Wyib sl1, k2tog, remove marker, brRsl, wyib sl1. (4 sts)

Row 80 (RS Color A): K1, k2tog, k1. (3 sts)

Row 81 (RS Color A): Wyib sl1, k2tog, psso.

Cut yarn and draw through remaining st.

Weave in ends and wet block to set sts.

DOE EARS BANDANA COWL

This stylish unisex cowl is worked using a repetition of brioche increases and decreases to create an intricate pattern. The cowl starts top down in the round and then is separated and shaped flat.

MATERIALS

- Color A: 140yd (128m) sport (4ply) weight yarn
  (Sample: Farmers Daughter Fibers, Recollect Sport in Daddy State of Mind)
- Color B: 165yd (151m) sport (4ply) weight yarn
  (Sample: Farmers Daughter Fibers, Recollect Sport in Legend)
- US 4 (3.5mm), 16in (40cm) circular needles
- 1 stitch marker

GAUGE (TENSION)

17 sts x 24 rows = 4in (10cm) in two-color brioche stitch on US 4 (3.5mm) needles, or size needed to obtain gauge.

MEASUREMENTS

24in (61cm) around x 14in (35.5cm) at longest point, very stretchy

NOTE

When knitting brioche flat, remember it takes two passes to equal a row. To be more specific, on a RS row you will work the first pass [brk] in Color A, then slide the stitches up to work the second pass [brp] in color B, completing one RS row. You'll know you have finished both passes of a row when the A/B yarns are on the right needle ready to be turned for the WS row. You'll repeat this for the WS row with stitches reversed, Color A [brp] and color B [brk], turning to work RS after both passes are complete.

ABBREVIATIONS

brk	Brioche knit: knit slipped stitch together with its yarn over
brkyobrk	A 2-stitch increase in brioche knit: brioche knit, yarn over, brioche knit into the same stitch
brLsl	A 2-stitch decrease that slants to the left, involving three stitches: slip the first stitch knitwise, brk the following two stitches together, pass the slipped stitch over
brRsl	A 2-stitch decrease that slants to the right, involving three stitches) = slip the first stitch knitwise, knit the next stitch, pass the slipped stitch over, place stitch on left hand needle and pass the following stitch over. Place stitch back on right hand needle
brp	Brioche purl: purl slipped stitch together with its yarn over
CO	Cast on
k	Knit stitch
k2tog	Knit 2 stitches together
p	Purl stitch
PM	Place marker
psso	Pass slipped stitch over
sl	Slip 1 stitch purlwise
sl1yo	With yarn in front, slip 1 stitch purlwise, yarn over
wyib/wyif	With yarn in back / With yarn in front

INSTRUCTIONS

Using US 4 (3.5mm) needles and Color B, CO 98 sts.

Being careful not to twist sts, PM and join in the round.

Round 1: K to end of round.

Round 2 (Color A): *Sl1yo, k1; repeat from * to end of round.

Round 2 (Color B): *Brp, sl1yo; repeat from * to end of round.

Round 3 (Color A): *Sl1yo, brk; repeat from * to end of round.

Round 3 (Color B): *Brp, sl1yo; repeat from * to end of round.

Round 4 (Color A): [Sl1yo, brk] twice, sl1yo, *brkyobrk, sl1yo, brkyobrk, sl1yo, [brk, sl1yo] 5 times; repeat from * to last 9 sts, brkyobrk, sl1yo, brkyobrk, [sl1yo, brk] 3 times. (126 sts)

Round 4 (Color B): Brp, [sl1yo, brp] twice, *sl1yo, p1, sl1yo, brp, sl1yo, p1, sl1yo, brp, [sl1yo, brp] 5 times; repeat from * to last 13 sts, sl1yo, p1, sl1yo, brp, sl1yo, p1, sl1yo, [brp, sl1yo] 3 times.

Round 5 (Color A): *Sl1yo, brk; repeat from * to end of round.

Round 5 (Color B): *Brp, sl1yo; repeat from * to end of round.

Round 6 (Color A): Sl1yo, brk, sl1yo, *brLsl, sl1yo, brk, sl1yo, brk, sl1yo, brRsl, sl1yo, [brk, sl1yo] 3 times; repeat from * to last 15 sts, brLsl, sl1yo, brk, sl1yo, brk, sl1yo, brRsl, sl1yo, brk, sl1yo, brk. (98 sts)

Round 6 (Color B): *Brp, sl1yo; repeat from * to end of round.

Round 7 (Color A): *Sl1yo, brk; repeat from * to end of round.

Round 7 (Color B): *Brp, sl1yo; repeat from * to end of round.

Repeat Rounds 4 to 7 eight more times.

Round 40 (Color A): [Sl1yo, brk] 3 times, sl1yo, brkyobrk, sl1yo, [brk, sl1yo] 5 times, *brkyobrk, sl1yo, brkyobrk, sl1yo, [brk, sl1yo] 5 times; repeat from * to last 9 sts, brkyobrk, [sl1yo, brk] 4 times. (122 sts)

Round 40 (Color B): Brp, [sl1yo, brp] 3 times, sl1yo, p1, sl1yo, [brp, sl1yo] 5 times, brp, *sl1yo, p1, sl1yo, brp, sl1yo, p1, sl1yo, brp, [sl1yo, brp] 5 times; repeat from * to last 11 sts, sl1yo, p1, sl1yo, [brp, sl1yo] three times, brp, k1, pass last worked brp over. (121 sts)

Remove marker and turn to work WS, you will now be working flat.

Row 41 (WS Color A): Wyif sl1, *brp, sl1yo; repeat from * to last 2 sts, brp, wyif sl1.

Row 41 (WS Color B): K1, *sl1yo, brk; repeat from * to last 2 sts, sl1yo, k1.

Row 42 (RS Color A): Wyib sl1, brLsl, [sl1yo, brk] twice, sl1yo, brRsl, sl1yo, [brk, sl1yo] 3 times, *brLsl, sl1yo, brk, sl1yo, brk, sl1yo, brRsl, sl1yo, [brk, sl1yo] 3 times; repeat from * to last 12 sts, brLsl, sl1yo, brk, sl1yo, brk, sl1yo, brRsl, wyib sl1. (93 sts)

Row 42 (RS Color B): K1, *sl1yo, brp; repeat from * to last 2 sts, sl1yo, k1.

Row 43 (WS Color A): Wyif sl1, *brp, sl1yo; repeat from * to last 2 sts, brp, wyif sl1.

Row 43 (WS Color B): K1, *sl1yo, brk; repeat from * to last 2 sts, sl1yo, k1.

Row 44 (RS Color A): Wyib sl1, brLsl, sl1yo, brkyobrk, [sl1yo, brk] 4 times, sl1yo, *brk, sl1yo, brkyobrk, sl1yo, brkyobrk, [sl1yo, brk] 4 times, sl1yo; repeat from * to last 8 sts, brk, sl1yo, brkyobrk, sl1yo, brRsl, wyib sl1. (113 sts)

Row 44 (RS Color B): K1, sl1yo, brp, sl1yo, p1, sl1yo, *[brp, sl1yo] 6 times, p1, sl1yo, brp, sl1yo, p1, sl1yo; repeat from * to last 17 sts, [brp, sl1yo] 6 times, p1, sl1yo, brp, sl1yo, k1.

Row 45 (WS Color A): Wyif sl1, *brp, sl1yo; repeat from * to last 2 sts, brp, wyif sl1.

Row 45 (WS Color B): K1, *sl1yo, brk; repeat from * to last 2 sts, sl1yo, k1.

Row 46 (RS Color A): Wyib sl1, brLsl, sl1yo, brRsl, sl1yo, [brk, sl1yo] 3 times, *brLsl, sl1yo, brk, sl1yo, brk, sl1yo, brRsl, sl1yo, [brk, sl1yo] 3 times; repeat from * to last 8 sts, brLsl, sl1yo, brRsl, wyib sl1. (85 sts)

Row 46 (RS Color B): K1, *sl1yo, brp; repeat from * to last 2 sts, sl1yo, k1.

Row 47 (WS Color A): Wyif sl1, *brp, sl1yo; repeat from * to last 2 sts, brp, wyif sl1.

Row 47 (WS Color B): K1, *sl1yo, brk; repeat from * to last 2 sts, sl1yo, k1.

Row 48 (RS Color A): Wyib sl1, brLsl, [sl1yo, brk] 3 times, sl1yo, *brk, sl1yo, brkyobrk, sl1yo, brkyobrk, [sl1yo, brk] 4 times, sl1yo; repeat from * to last 4 sts, brRsl, wyib sl1. (101 sts)

Row 48 (RS Color B): K1, [sl1yo, brp] 5 times, sl1yo, *p1, sl1yo, brp, sl1yo, p1, sl1yo, [brp, sl1yo] 6 times; repeat from * to last 17 sts, p1, sl1yo, brp, sl1yo, p1, sl1yo, [brp, sl1yo] 5 times, k1.

Row 49 (WS Color A): Wyif sl1, *brp, sl1yo; repeat from * to last 2 sts, brp, wyif sl1.

Row 49 (WS Color B): K1, *sl1yo, brk; repeat from * to last 2 sts, sl1yo, k1.

Row 50 (RS Color A): Wyib sl1, brLsl, sl1yo, [brk, sl1yo] twice, *brLsl, sl1yo, brk, sl1yo, brk, sl1yo, brRsl, sl1yo, [brk, sl1yo] 3 times; repeat from * to last 20 sts, brLsl, sl1yo, brk, sl1yo, brk, sl1yo, brRsl, sl1yo, [brk, sl1yo] twice, brRsl, wyib sl1. (77 sts)

Row 50 (RS Color B): K1, *sl1yo, brp; repeat from * to last 2 sts, sl1yo, k1.

Row 51 (WS Color A): Wyif sl1, *brp, sl1yo; repeat from * to last 2 sts, brp, wyif sl1.

Row 51 (WS Color B): K1, *sl1yo, brk; repeat from * to last 2 sts, sl1yo, k1.

Row 52 (RS Color A): Wyib sl1, brLsl, sl1yo, brk, sl1yo, *brk, sl1yo, brkyobrk, sl1yo, brkyobrk, [sl1yo, brk] 4 times, sl1yo; repeat from * to last 14 sts, brk, sl1yo, brkyobrk, sl1yo, brkyobrk, [sl1yo, brk] twice, sl1yo, brRsl, wyib sl1. (93 sts)

Row 52 (RS Color B): K1, [sl1yo, brp] 3 times, sl1yo, *p1, sl1yo, brp, sl1yo, p1, sl1yo, [brp, sl1yo] 6 times; repeat from * to last 13 sts, p1, sl1yo, brp, sl1yo, p1, sl1yo, [brp, sl1yo] 3 times, k1.

Row 53 (WS Color A): Wyif sl1, *brp, sl1yo; repeat from * to last 2 sts, brp, wyif sl1.

Row 53 (WS Color B): K1, *sl1yo, brk; repeat from * to last 2 sts, sl1yo, k1.

Row 54 (RS Color A): Wyib sl1, brLsl, sl1yo, *brLsl, sl1yo, brk, sl1yo, brk, sl1yo, brRsl, sl1yo, [brk, sl1yo] 3 times; repeat from * to last 16 sts, brLsl, sl1yo, brk, sl1yo, brk, sl1yo, brRsl, sl1yo, brRsl, wyib sl1. (69 sts)

Row 54 (RS Color B): K1, *sl1yo, brp; repeat from * to last 2 sts, sl1yo, k1.

Row 55 (WS Color A): Wyif sl1, *brp, sl1yo; repeat from * to last 2 sts, brp, wyif sl1.

Row 55 (WS Color B): K1, *sl1yo, brk; repeat from * to last 2 sts, sl1yo, k1.

Row 56 (RS Color A): Wyib sl1, brLsl, sl1yo, brk, sl1yo, brkyobrk, sl1yo, brk, *[sl1yo, brk] 4 times, sl1yo, brkyobrk, sl1yo, brkyobrk, sl1yo, brk; repeat from * to last 17 sts, [sl1yo, brk] 4 times, sl1yo, brkyobrk, sl1yo, brk, sl1yo, brRsl, wyib sl1. (81 sts)

Row 56 (RS Color B): K1, [sl1yo, brp] twice, sl1yo, p1, sl1yo, [brp, sl1yo] 6 times, *p1, sl1yo, brp, sl1yo, p1, sl1yo, [brp, sl1yo] 6 times; repeat from * to last 7 sts, p1, [sl1yo, brp] twice, sl1yo, k1.

Row 57 (WS Color A): Wyif sl1, *brp, sl1yo; repeat from * to last 2 sts, brp, wyif sl1.

Row 57 (WS Color B): K1, *sl1yo, brk; repeat from * to last 2 sts, sl1yo, k1.

Row 58 (RS Color A): Wyib sl1, brLsl, sl1yo, brk, sl1yo, brRsl, [sl1yo, brk] 3 times, sl1yo, *brLsl, sl1yo, brk, sl1yo, brk, sl1yo, brRsl, sl1yo, [brk, sl1yo] 3 times; repeat from * to last 10 sts, brLsl, sl1yo, brk, sl1yo, brRsl, wyib sl1. (61 sts)

Row 58 (RS Color B): K1, *sl1yo, brp; repeat from * to last 2 sts, sl1yo, k1.

Row 59 (WS Color A): Wyif sl1, *brp, sl1yo; repeat from * to last 2 sts, brp, wyif sl1.

Row 59 (WS Color B): K1, *sl1yo, brk; repeat from * to last 2 sts, sl1yo, k1.

Row 60 (RS Color A): Wyib sl1, brLsl, sl1yo, brk, *[sl1yo, brk] 4 times, sl1yo, brkyobrk, sl1yo, brkyobrk, sl1yo, brk; repeat from * to last 13 sts, [sl1yo, brk] 4 times, sl1yo, brRsl, wyib sl1. (69 sts)

Row 60 (RS Color B): K1, sl1yo, *[brp, sl1yo] 6 times, p1, sl1yo, brp, sl1yo, p1, sl1yo; repeat from * to last 13 sts, [brp, sl1yo] 6 times, k1.

Row 61 (WS Color A): Wyif sl1, *brp, sl1yo; repeat from * to last 2 sts, brp, wyif sl1.

Row 61 (WS Color B): K1, *sl1yo, brk; repeat from * to last 2 sts, sl1yo, k1.

Row 62 (RS Color A): Wyib sl1, brLsl, [sl1yo, brk] 3 times, sl1yo, *brLsl, sl1yo, brk, sl1yo, brk, sl1yo, brRsl, sl1yo, [brk, sl1yo] 3 times; repeat from * to last 4 sts, brRsl, wyib sl1. (53 sts)

Row 62 (RS Color B): K1, *sl1yo, brp; repeat from * to last 2 sts, sl1yo, k1.

Row 63 (WS Color A): Wyif sl1, *brp, sl1yo; repeat from * to last 2 sts, brp, wyif sl1.

Row 63 (WS Color B): K1, *sl1yo, brk; repeat from * to last 2 sts, sl1yo, k1.

Row 64 (RS Color A): Wyib sl1, brLsl, [sl1yo, brk] 3 times, *sl1yo, brkyobrk, sl1yo, brkyobrk, [sl1yo, brk] 5 times; repeat from * to last 15 sts, sl1yo, brkyobrk, sl1yo, brkyobrk, [sl1yo, brk] 3 times, sl1yo, brRsl, wyib sl1. (61 sts)

Row 64 (RS Color B): K1, [sl1yo, brp] 3 times, sl1yo, *brp, sl1yo, p1, sl1yo, brp, sl1yo, p1, sl1yo, [brp, sl1yo] 5 times; repeat from * to last 17 sts, brp, sl1yo, p1, sl1yo, brp, sl1yo, p1, sl1yo, [brp, sl1yo] 4 times, k1.

Row 65 (WS Color A): Wyif sl1, *brp, sl1yo; repeat from * to last 2 sts, brp, wyif sl1.

Row 65 (WS Color B): K1, *sl1yo, brk; repeat from * to last 2 sts, sl1yo, k1.

Row 66 (RS Color A): Wyib sl1, brLsl, sl1yo, brk, sl1yo, *brLsl, sl1yo, brk, sl1yo, brk, sl1yo, brRsl, sl1yo, [brk, sl1yo] 3 times; repeat from * to last 18 sts, brLsl, sl1yo, brk, sl1yo, brk, sl1yo, brRsl, sl1yo, brk, sl1yo, brRsl, wyib sl1. (45 sts)

Row 66 (RS Color B): K1, *sl1yo, brp; repeat from * to last 2 sts, sl1yo, k1.

Row 67 (WS Color A): Wyif sl1, *brp, sl1yo; repeat from * to last 2 sts, brp, wyif sl1.

Row 67 (WS Color B): K1, *sl1yo, brk; repeat from * to last 2 sts, sl1yo, k1.

Row 68 (RS Color A): Wyib sl1, brLsl, [sl1yo, brk] twice, sl1yo, brkyobrk, [sl1yo, brk] 5 times, sl1yo, brkyobrk, sl1yo, brkyobrk, [sl1yo, brk] 5 times, sl1yo, brkyobrk, [sl1yo, brk] twice, sl1yo, brRsl, wyib sl1. (49 sts)

Row 68 (RS Color B): K1, [sl1yo, brp] 3 times, sl1yo, p1, sl1yo, brp, [sl1yo, brp] 5 times, sl1yo, p1, sl1yo, brp, sl1yo, p1, sl1yo, brp, [sl1yo, brp] 5 times, sl1yo, p1, sl1yo, [brp, sl1yo] 3 times, k1.

Row 69 (WS Color A): Wyif sl1, *brp, sl1yo; repeat from * to last 2 sts, brp, wyif sl1.

Row 69 (WS Color B): K1, *sl1yo, brk; repeat from * to last 2 sts, sl1yo, k1.

Row 70 (RS Color A): Wyib sl1, brLsl, [sl1yo, brk] twice, sl1yo, brRsl, sl1yo, [brk, sl1yo] 3 times, brLsl, [sl1yo, brk] twice, sl1yo, brRsl, sl1yo, [brk, sl1yo] 3 times, brLsl, [sl1yo, brk] twice, sl1yo, brRsl, wyib sl1. (37 sts)

Row 70 (RS Color B): K1, *sl1yo, brp; repeat from * to last 2 sts, sl1yo, k1.

Row 71 (WS Color A): Wyif sl1, *brp, sl1yo; repeat from * to last 2 sts, brp, wyif sl1.

Row 71 (WS Color B): K1, *sl1yo, brk; repeat from * to last 2 sts, sl1yo, k1.

Row 72 (RS Color A): Wyib sl1, brLsl, [sl1yo, brk] 6 times, sl1yo, brkyobrk, sl1yo, brkyobrk, [sl1yo, brk] 6 times, sl1yo, brRsl, wyib sl1. (37 sts)

Row 72 (RS Color B): K1, [sl1yo, brp] 7 times, sl1yo, p1, sl1yo, brp, sl1yo, p1, sl1yo, [brp, sl1yo] 7 times, k1.

Row 73 (WS Color A): Wyif sl1, *brp, sl1yo; repeat from * to last 2 sts, brp, wyif sl1.

Row 73 (WS Color B): K1, *sl1yo, brk; repeat from * to last 2 sts, sl1yo, k1.

Row 74 (RS Color A): Wyib sl1, brLsl, [sl1yo, brk] 4 times, sl1yo, brLsl, [sl1yo, brk] twice, sl1yo, brRsl, sl1yo, [brk, sl1yo] 4 times, brRsl, wyib sl1. (29 sts)

Row 74 (RS Color B): K1, *sl1yo, brp; repeat from * to last 2 sts, sl1yo, k1.

Row 75 (WS Color A): Wyif sl1, *brp, sl1yo; repeat from * to last 2 sts, brp, wyif sl1.

Row 75 (WS Color B): K1, *sl1yo, brk; repeat from * to last 2 sts, sl1yo, k1.

Row 76 (RS Color A): Wyib sl1, brLsl, [sl1yo, brk] 4 times, sl1yo, brkyobrk, sl1yo, brkyobrk, [sl1yo, brk] 4 times, sl1yo, brRsl, wyib sl1. (29 sts)

Row 76 (RS Color B): K1, [sl1yo, brp] 5 times, sl1yo, p1, sl1yo, brp, sl1yo, p1, sl1yo, [brp, sl1yo] 5 times, k1.

Row 77 (WS Color A): Wyif sl1, *brp, sl1yo; repeat from * to last 2 sts, brp, wyif sl1.

Row 77 (WS Color B): K1, *sl1yo, brk; repeat from * to last 2 sts, sl1yo, k1.

Row 78 (RS Color A): Wyib sl1, brLsl, [sl1yo, brk] twice, sl1yo, brLsl, [sl1yo, brk] twice, sl1yo, brRsl, sl1yo, [brk, sl1yo] twice, brRsl, wyib sl1. (21 sts)

Row 78 (RS Color B): K1, *sl1yo, brp; repeat from * to last 2 sts, sl1yo, k1.

Row 79 (WS Color A): Wyif sl1, *brp, sl1yo; repeat from * to last 2 sts, brp, wyif sl1.

Row 79 (WS Color B): K1, *sl1yo, brk; repeat from * to last 2 sts, sl1yo, k1.

Row 80 (RS Color A): Wyib sl1, brLsl, [sl1yo, brk] twice, sl1yo, brkyobrk, sl1yo, brkyobrk, [sl1yo, brk] twice, sl1yo, brRsl, wyib sl1. (21 sts)

Row 80 (RS Color B): K1, [sl1yo, brp] 3 times, sl1yo, p1, sl1yo, brp, sl1yo, p1, sl1yo, [brp, sl1yo] 3 times, k1.

Row 81 (WS Color A): Wyif sl1, *brp, sl1yo; repeat from * to last 2 sts, brp, wyif sl1.

Row 81 (WS Color B): K1, *sl1yo, brk; repeat from * to last 2 sts, sl1yo, k1.

Row 82 (RS Color A): Wyib sl1, brLsl, sl1yo, brLsl, [sl1yo, brk] twice, sl1yo, brRsl, sl1yo, brRsl, wyib sl1. (13 sts)

Row 82 (RS Color B): K1, *sl1yo, brp; repeat from * to last 2 sts, sl1yo, k1.

Row 83 (WS Color A): Wyif sl1, *brp, sl1yo; repeat from * to last 2 sts, brp, wyif sl1.

Row 83 (WS Color B): K1, *sl1yo, brk; repeat from * to last 2 sts, sl1yo, k1.

Row 84 (RS Color A): Wyib sl1, brLsl, sl1yo, brk, sl1yo, brk, sl1yo, brRsl, wyib sl1. (9 sts)

Row 84 (RS Color B): K1, *sl1yo, brp; repeat from * to last 2 sts, sl1yo, k1.

Row 85 (WS Color A): Wyif sl1, *brp, sl1yo; repeat from * to last 2 sts, brp, wyif sl1.

Row 85 (WS Color B): K1, *sl1yo, brk; repeat from * to last 2 sts, sl1yo, k1.

Row 86 (RS Color A): Wyib sl1, brLsl, sl1yo, brRsl, wyib sl1. (5 sts)

Row 86 (RS Color B): K1, sl1yo, brp, sl1yo, k1.

Row 87 (WS Color A): Wyif sl1, brp, sl1yo, brp, wyif sl1.

Row 87 (WS Color B): K1, sl1yo, brk, sl1yo, k1.

Row 88 (RS Color A): Wyib sl1, brRsl, wyib sl1. (3 sts)

Row 88 (RS Color B): Sl1, k2tog, psso, break yarn and pull through remaining st.

Weave in ends and wet block to set sts.

PEACH BLOSSOM HAT

This slouch hat in bulky (chunky) yarn was inspired by flower buds. The use of increases and decreases creates a pretty motif and looks like a flower opening at the crown shaping.

MATERIALS

- Color A: 85yd (78m) bulky (chunky) weight yarn *(Sample: Manos Del Uruguay, Cardo in Peach Blossom)*
- Color B: 75yd (69m) bulky (chunky) weight yarn *(Sample: Manos Del Uruguay, Cardo in Sword)*
- US 8 (5mm), 16in (40cm) circular needles
- US 8 (5mm) double-pointed needles (DPNs)
- 1 stitch marker

GAUGE (TENSION)

12 sts x 16 rows = 4in (10cm) in two-color brioche stitch on US 8 (5mm) needles, or size needed to obtain gauge.

MEASUREMENTS

Measurements: 20 x 9½in (51 x 24cm)

Hat will fit up to a 24in (61cm) head circumference.

ABBREVIATIONS

brk	Brioche knit: knit slipped stitch together with its yarn over
brkyobrk	A 2-stitch increase in brioche knit: brioche knit, yarn over, brioche knit into the same stitch
brLsl	A 2-stitch decrease that slants to the left, involving three stitches: slip the first stitch knitwise, brk the following two stitches together, pass the slipped stitch over
brRsl	A 2-stitch decrease that slants to the right, involving three stitches: slip the first stitch knitwise, knit the next stitch, pass the slipped stitch over, place stitch on left hand needle and pass the following stitch over. Place stitch back on right hand needle
brp	Brioche purl: purl slipped stitch together with its yarn over
CO	Cast on
k	Knit stitch
k2tog	Knit 2 stitches together
p	Purl stitch
PM	Place marker
sl1	Slip 1 stitch purlwise
sl1yo	With yarn in front, slip 1 stitch purlwise, yarn over

INSTRUCTIONS

Using US 8 (5mm) circular needles and Color A, CO 60 sts.

Being careful not to twist sts, PM and join in the round.

Round 1-10: *P1, k1; repeat from * to end of round.

Round 11 (Color A): *Sl1yo, k1; repeat from * to end of round.

Round 11 (Color B): *Brp, sl1yo; repeat from * to end of round.

Round 12 (Color A): *Sl1yo, brk; repeat from * to end of round.

Round 12 (Color B): *Brp, sl1yo; repeat from * to end of round.

Round 13 (Color A): *Sl1yo, brk; repeat from * to end of round.

Round 13 (Color B): *Brp, sl1yo; repeat from * to end of round.

Round 14 (Color A): *Sl1yo, brk; repeat from * to end of round.

Round 14 (Color B): *Brp, sl1yo; repeat from * to end of round.

Round 15 (Color A): *Sl1yo, [brk, sl1yo] twice, brkyobrk, sl1yo, brkyobrk, sl1yo, brk; repeat from * to end of round. (84 sts)

Round 15 (Color B): *Brp, [sl1yo, brp] twice, sl1yo, p1, sl1yo, brp, sl1yo, p1, sl1yo, brp, sl1yo; repeat from * to end of round.

Round 16 (Color A): *Sl1yo, brk; repeat from * to end of round.

Round 16 (Color B): *brp, sl1yo; repeat from * to end of round

Round 17 (Color A): *Sl1yo, brk; repeat from * to end of round.

Round 17 (Color B): *Brp, sl1yo; repeat from * to end of round.

Round 18 (Color A): *Sl1yo, brk, sl1yo, brLsl, [sl1yo, brk] 2 times, sl1yo, brRsl; repeat from * to end of round. (60 sts)

Round 18 (Color B): *Brp, sl1yo; repeat from * to end of round.

Round 19 (Color A): *Sl1yo, brk; repeat from * to end of round.

Round 19 (Color B): *Brp, sl1yo; repeat from * to end of round.

Work Rounds 15 to 19 three more times.

BEGIN CROWN SHAPING:

Round 35 (Color A): *Sl1yo, brk; repeat from * to end of round.

Round 35 (Color B): *Brp, sl1yo; repeat from * to end of round.

Round 36 (Color A): *Sl1yo, brk, sl1yo, brLsl, sl1yo, brRsl; repeat from * to end of round. (36 sts)

Round 36 (Color B): *Brp, sl1yo; repeat from * to end of round.

Round 37 (Color A): *Sl1yo, brk; repeat from * to end of round.

Round 37 (Color B): *Brp, sl1yo; repeat from * to end of round.

Switch to DPNs.

Round 38 (Color A): *Sl1yo, brk, sl1yo, brRsl; repeat from * to end of round. (24 sts)

Round 38 (Color B): *Brp, sl1yo; repeat from * to end of round.

Round 39 (Color A): *Sl1yo, brk; repeat from * to end of round.

Round 39 (Color B): *Brp, sl1yo; repeat from * to end of round.

Round 40 (Color A): *Sl1yo, brLsl, sl1yo, brRsl; repeat from * to end of round. (12 sts)

Round 40 (Color B): *Brp, sl1yo; repeat from * to end of round.

Break Color B.

Round 41 (Color A): *K1, brk; repeat from * to end of round.

Round 42 (Color A): *K2tog; repeat from * to end of round. (6 sts)

Cut tail draw through remaining sts and fasten off.

Weave in ends and wet block to set sts.

RESIDENTS SHAWL

IIIIIIIIIIIIIII

This crescent-shaped shawl uses just two skeins of fingering (2ply) weight yarn to knit a fun syncopated brioche pattern. The optional fringe makes for a fun blend of textures and a very fancy shawl for spring!

MATERIALS

- Color A: 400yd (366m) fingering (2ply) weight yarn
  (Sample: The Farmer's Daughter Fibers, Foxy Lady in Coal Miner's Daughter)
- Color B: 400yd (366m) fingering (2ply) weight yarn
  (Sample: The Farmer's Daughter Fibers, Foxy Lady in Reservation Remix)
- US 4 (3.5mm), 40in (100cm) circular needles
- 2 stitch markers
- Crochet hook (to attach fringe)

GAUGE (TENSION)

12 sts x 32 rows = 4in (10cm) in two-color brioche stitch on US 4 (3.5mm) needles, or size needed to obtain gauge.

MEASUREMENTS

70in (178cm) wingspan, 14in (35.5cm) long (18in / 45.5cm long with fringe)

NOTES

When knitting brioche flat, remember it takes two passes to equal a row. To be more specific, on a RS row you will work the first pass [brk] in Color B, then slide the stitches up to work the second pass [brp] in Color A, completing one RS row. You'll know you have finished both passes of a row when the A/B yarns are on the right needle ready to be turned for the WS row. You'll repeat this for the WS row with stitches reversed, Color B [brp] and Color A [brk], turning to work RS after both passes are complete.

This project uses a yarn over bind (cast) off for a stretchy edge – see step-by-step instructions for how to work this in the General Techniques section.

ABBREVIATIONS

brk	Brioche knit: knit slipped stitch together with its yarn over
brp	Brioche purl: purl slipped stitch together with its yarn over
brkyobrk	A 2-stitch increase in brioche knit: brioche knit, yarn over, brioche knit into the same stitch
brpyobrp	A 2-stitch increase in brioche purl: brioche purl, yarn over, brioche purl into the same stitch
CO	Cast on using the knit on method
k	Knit stitch
kyok	Knit, yarn over, knit into the same stitch
k2tog	Knit 2 stitches together
p	Purl stitch
PM / SM	Place marker / slide marker
sl1yo	With yarn in front, slip 1 stitch purlwise, yarn over
yo	Yarn over

INSTRUCTIONS

Using US 4 (3.5mm) needles and Color A, CO 3 sts.

Rows 1 to 6: K to end of row.

Row 7: Pick up and k 3 sts along garter edge, pick up and k 3 sts along cast-on edge. (9 sts)

Row 8: K3, PM, kyok, k to last 4 sts, kyok, PM, k3. (13 sts)

Row 9 (RS Color B): K3, SM, kyok, sl1yo, k1, sl1yo, k1, sl1yo, kyok, SM, k3. (17 sts)

Row 9 (RS Color A): P3, SM, sl1yo, p1, sl1yo, brp, sl1yo, brp, sl1yo, brp, sl1yo, p1, sl1yo, SM, p3.

Row 10 (WS Color B): P3, SM, brp, *sl1yo, brp; repeat from * to marker, SM, p3.

Row 10 (WS Color A): K3, SM, sl1yo, *brk, sl1yo; repeat from * to marker, SM, k3.

BEGIN SYNCOPATED BRIOCHE:

> *NOTE: You will now be alternating between starting your RS rows with brk or starting them with brp to create a syncopated brioche, or broken rib. Be sure to keep track of your rows.*

Row 11 (RS Color A): K3, SM, brpyobrp, *sl1yo, brp; repeat from * to last 5 sts, sl1yo, brpyobrp, SM, k3. (21 sts)

Row 11 (RS Color B): P3, SM, sl1yo, k1, sl1yo, *brk, sl1yo; repeat from * to last 7 sts, brk, sl1yo, k1, sl1yo, SM, p3.

Row 12 (WS Color A): P3, SM, brk, *sl1yo, brk; repeat from * to marker, SM, p3.

Row 12 (WS Color B): K3, SM, sl1yo, *brp, sl1yo; repeat from * to marker, SM, k3.

Row 13 (RS Color B): K3, SM, brkyobrk, *sl1yo, brk; repeat from * to last 5 sts, sl1yo, brkyobrk, SM, k3. (25 sts)

Row 13 (RS Color A): P3, SM, sl1yo, p1, sl1yo, *brp, sl1yo; repeat from * to last 7 sts, brp, sl1yo, p1, sl1yo, SM, p3.

Row 14 (WS Color B): P3, SM, brp, *sl1yo, brp; repeat from * to marker, SM, p3

Row 14 (WS Color A): K3, SM, sl1yo, *brk, sl1yo; repeat from * to marker, SM, k3.

Row 15 (RS Color A): K3, SM, brpyobrp, *sl1yo, brp; repeat from * to last 5 sts, sl1yo, brpyobrp, SM, k3. (29 sts)

Row 15 (RS Color B): P3, SM, sl1yo, k1, sl1yo, *brk, sl1yo; repeat from * to last 7 sts, brk, sl1yo, k1, sl1yo, SM, p3.

Row 16 (WS Color A): P3, SM, brk, *sl1yo, brk; repeat from * to marker, SM, p3.

Row 16 (WS Color B): K3, SM, sl1yo, *brp, sl1yo; repeat from * to marker, SM, k3.

Row 17 (RS Color B): K3, SM, brkyobrk, *sl1yo, brk; repeat from * to last 5 sts, sl1yo, brkyobrk, SM, k3.

Row 17 (RS Color A): P3, SM, sl1yo, p1, sl1yo, *brp, sl1yo; repeat from * to last 7 sts, brp, sl1yo, p1, sl1yo, SM, p3.

Row 18 (WS Color B): P3, SM, brp, *sl1yo, brp; repeat from * to marker, SM, p3.

Row 18 (WS Color A): K3, SM, sl1yo, *brk, sl1yo; repeat from * to marker, SM, k3.

Repeat Rows 17 and 18 one more time. (37 sts)

Row 21 (RS Color A): K3, SM, brpyobrp, *sl1yo, brp; repeat from * to last 5 sts, sl1yo, brpyobrp, SM, k3.

Row 21 (RS Color B): P3, SM, sl1yo, k1, sl1yo, *brk, sl1yo; repeat from * to last 7 sts, brk, sl1yo, k1, sl1yo, SM, p3.

Row 22 (WS Color A): P3, SM, brk, *sl1yo, brk; repeat from * to marker, SM, p3.

Row 22 (WS Color B): K3, SM, sl1yo, *brp, sl1yo; repeat from * to marker, SM, k3.

Repeat Rows 21 and 22 one more time. (45 sts)

Row 25 (RS Color B): K3, SM, brkyobrk, *sl1yo, brk; repeat from * to last 5 sts, sl1yo, brkyobrk, SM, k3.

Row 25 (RS Color A): P3, SM, sl1yo, p1, sl1yo, *brp, sl1yo; repeat from * to last 7 sts, brp, sl1yo, p1, sl1yo, SM, p3.

Row 26 (WS Color B): P3, SM, brp, *sl1yo, brp; repeat from * to marker, SM, p3.

Row 26 (WS Color A): K3, SM, sl1yo, *brk, sl1yo; repeat from * to marker, SM, k3.

Repeat Rows 25 and 26 one more time. (53 sts)

Row 29 (RS Color A): K3, SM, brpyobrp, *sl1yo, brp; repeat from * to last 5 sts, sl1yo, brpyobrp, SM, k3.

Row 29 (RS Color B): P3, SM, sl1yo, k1, sl1yo, *brk, sl1yo; repeat from * to last 7 sts, brk, sl1yo, k1, sl1yo, SM, p3.

Row 30 (WS Color A): P3, SM, brk, *sl1yo, brk; repeat from * to marker, SM, p3.

Row 30 (WS Color B): K3, SM, sl1yo, *brp, sl1yo; repeat from * to marker, SM, k3.

Repeat Rows 29 and 30 one more time. (61 sts)

Row 33 (RS Color B): K3, SM, brkyobrk, *sl1yo, brk; repeat from * to last 5 sts, sl1yo, brkyobrk, SM, k3.

Row 33 (RS Color A): P3, SM, sl1yo, p1, sl1yo, *brp, sl1yo; repeat from * to last 7 sts, brp, sl1yo, p1, sl1yo, SM, p3.

Row 34 (WS Color B): P3, SM, brp, *sl1yo, brp; repeat from * to marker, SM, p3.

Row 34 (WS Color A): K3, SM, sl1yo, *brk, sl1yo; repeat from * to marker, SM, k3.

Repeat Rows 33 and 34 one more time. (69 sts)

Row 37 (RS Color A): K3, SM, brpyobrp, *sl1yo, brp; repeat from * to last 5 sts, sl1yo, brpyobrp, SM, k3.

Row 37 (RS Color B): P3, SM, sl1yo, k1, sl1yo, *brk, sl1yo; repeat from * to last 7 sts, brk, sl1yo, k1, sl1yo, SM, p3.

Row 38 (WS Color A): P3, SM, brk, *sl1yo, brk; repeat from * to marker, SM, p3.

Row 38 (WS Color B): K3, SM, sl1yo, *brp, sl1yo; repeat from * to marker, SM, k3.

Repeat Rows 37 and 38 one more time. (77 sts)

Row 41 (RS Color B): K3, SM, brkyobrk, *sl1yo, brk; repeat from * to last 5 sts, sl1yo, brkyobrk, SM, k3.

Row 41 (RS Color A): P3, SM, sl1yo, p1, sl1yo, *brp, sl1yo; repeat from * to last 7 sts, brp, sl1yo, p1, sl1yo, SM, p3.

Row 42 (WS Color B): P3, SM, brp, *sl1yo, brp; repeat from * to marker, SM, p3.

Row 42 (WS Color A): K3, SM, sl1yo, *brk, sl1yo; repeat from * to marker, SM, k3.

Repeat Rows 41 and 42 twice more. (89 sts)

Row 47 (RS Color A): K3, SM, brpyobrp, *sl1yo, brp; repeat from * to last 5 sts, sl1yo, brpyobrp, SM, k3.

Row 47 (RS Color B): P3, SM, sl1yo, k1, sl1yo, *brk, sl1yo; repeat from * to last 7 sts, brk, sl1yo, k1, sl1yo, SM, p3.

Row 48 (WS Color A): P3, SM, brk, *sl1yo, brk; repeat from * to marker, SM, p3.

Row 48 (WS Color B): K3, SM, sl1yo, *brp, sl1yo; repeat from * to marker, SM, k3.

Repeat Rows 47 and 48 twice more. (101 sts)

Row 53 (RS Color B): K3, SM, brkyobrk, *sl1yo, brk; repeat from * to last 5 sts, sl1yo, brkyobrk, SM, k3.

Row 53 (RS Color A): P3, SM, sl1yo, p1, sl1yo, *brp, sl1yo; repeat from * to last 7 sts, brp, sl1yo, p1, sl1yo, SM, p3.

Row 54 (WS Color B): P3, SM, brp, *sl1yo, brp; repeat from * to marker, SM, p3.

Row 54 (WS Color A): K3, SM, sl1yo, *brk, sl1yo; repeat from * to marker, SM, k3.

Repeat Rows 53 and 54 twice more. (113 sts)

Row 59 (RS Color A): K3, SM, brpyobrp, *sl1yo, brp; repeat from * to last 5 sts, sl1yo, brpyobrp, SM, k3.

Row 59 (RS Color B): P3, SM, sl1yo, k1, sl1yo, *brk, sl1yo; repeat from * to last 7 sts, brk, sl1yo, k1, sl1yo, SM, p3.

Row 60 (WS Color A): P3, SM, brk, *sl1yo, brk; repeat from * to marker, SM, p3.

Row 60 (WS Color B): K3, SM, sl1yo, *brp, sl1yo; repeat from * to marker, SM, k3.

Repeat Rows 59 and 60 twice more. (125 sts)

Row 65 (RS Color B): K3, SM, brkyobrk, *sl1yo, brk; repeat from * to last 5 sts, sl1yo, brkyobrk, SM, k3.

Row 65 (RS Color A): P3, SM, sl1yo, p1, sl1yo, *brp, sl1yo; repeat from * to last 7 sts, brp, sl1yo, p1, sl1yo, SM, p3.

Row 66 (WS Color B): P3, SM, brp, *sl1yo, brp; repeat from * to marker, SM, p3.

Row 66 (WS Color A): K3, SM, sl1yo, *brk, sl1yo; repeat from * to marker, SM, k3.

Repeat Rows 65 and 66 twice more. (137 sts)

Row 71 (RS Color A): K3, SM, brpyobrp, *sl1yo, brp; repeat from * to last 5 sts, sl1yo, brpyobrp, SM, k3.

Row 71 (RS Color B): P3, SM, sl1yo, k1, sl1yo, *brk, sl1yo; repeat from * to last 7 sts, brk, sl1yo, k1, sl1yo, SM, p3.

Row 72 (WS Color A): P3, SM, brk, *sl1yo, brk; repeat from * to marker, SM, p3.

Row 72 (WS Color B): K3, SM, sl1yo, *brp, sl1yo; repeat from * to marker, SM, k3.

Repeat Rows 71 and 72 twice more. (149 sts)

Row 77 (RS Color B): K3, SM, brkyobrk, *sl1yo, brk; repeat from * to last 5 sts, sl1yo, brkyobrk, SM, k3.

Row 77 (RS Color A): P3, SM, sl1yo, p1, sl1yo, *brp, sl1yo; repeat from * to last 7 sts, brp, sl1yo, p1, sl1yo, SM, p3.

Row 78 (WS Color B): P3, SM, brp, *sl1yo, brp; repeat from * to marker, SM, p3.

Row 78 (WS Color A): K3, SM, sl1yo, *brk, sl1yo; repeat from * to marker, SM, k3.

Repeat Rows 77 and 78 three more times. (165 sts)

Row 85 (RS Color A): K3, SM, brpyobrp, *sl1yo, brp; repeat from * to last 5 sts, sl1yo, brpyobrp, SM, k3.

Row 85 (RS Color B): P3, SM, sl1yo, k1, sl1yo, *brk, sl1yo; repeat from * to last 7 sts, brk, sl1yo, k1, sl1yo, SM, p3.

Row 86 (WS Color A): P3, SM, brk, *sl1yo, brk; repeat from * to marker, SM, p3.

Row 86 (WS Color B): K3, SM, sl1yo, *brp, sl1yo; repeat from * to marker, SM, k3.

Repeat Rows 85 and 86 three more times. (181 sts)

Row 93 (RS Color B): K3, SM, brkyobrk, *sl1yo, brk; repeat from * to last 5 sts, sl1yo, brkyobrk, SM, k3.

Row 93 (RS Color A): P3, SM, sl1yo, p1, sl1yo, *brp, sl1yo; repeat from * to last 7 sts, brp, sl1yo, p1, sl1yo, SM, p3.

Row 94 (WS Color B): P3, SM, brp, *sl1yo, brp; repeat from * to marker, SM, p3.

Row 94 (WS Color A): K3, SM, sl1yo, *brk, sl1yo; repeat from * to marker, SM, k3.

Repeat Rows 93 and 94 three more times. (197 sts)

Row 101 (RS Color A): K3, SM, brpyobrp, *sl1yo, brp; repeat from * to last 5 sts, sl1yo, brpyobrp, SM, k3.

Row 101 (RS Color B): P3, SM, sl1yo, k1, sl1yo, *brk, sl1yo; repeat from * to last 7 sts, brk, sl1yo, k1, sl1yo, SM, p3.

Row 102 (WS Color A): P3, SM, brk, *sl1yo, brk; repeat from * to marker, SM, p3.

Row 102 (WS Color B): K3, SM, sl1yo, *brp, sl1yo; repeat from * to marker, SM, k3.

Repeat Rows 101 and 102 three more times. (213 sts)

Row 109 (RS Color B): K3, SM, brkyobrk, *sl1yo, brk; repeat from * to last 5 sts, sl1yo, brkyobrk, SM, k3.

Row 109 (RS Color A): P3, SM, sl1yo, p1, sl1yo, *brp, sl1yo; repeat from * to last 7 sts, brp, sl1yo, p1, sl1yo, SM, p3.

Row 110 (WS Color B): P3, SM, brp, *sl1yo, brp; repeat from * to marker, SM, p3.

Row 110 (WS Color A): K3, SM, sl1yo, *brk, sl1yo; repeat from * to marker, SM, k3.

Repeat Rows 109 and 110 three more times. (229 sts)

Row 117 (RS Color A): K3, SM, brpyobrp, *sl1yo, brp; repeat from * to last 5 sts, sl1yo, brpyobrp, SM, k3.

Row 117 (RS Color B): P3, SM, sl1yo, k1, sl1yo, *brk, sl1yo; repeat from * to last 7 sts, brk, sl1yo, k1, sl1yo, SM, p3.

Row 118 (WS Color A): P3, SM, brk, *sl1yo, brk; repeat from * to marker, SM, p3.

Row 118 (WS Color B): K3, SM, sl1yo, *brp, sl1yo; repeat from * to marker, SM, k3.

Repeat Rows 117 and 118 three more times. (245 sts)

Break Color A.

Row 125 (RS Color B): K3, *brk, k1; repeat from * to last 4 sts, brk, k3.

Using Color B, bind (cast) off as follows: K1, *yo purlwise, k1, pass yo and k stitch over last k st, repeat from * to end of row, cut yarn and draw through remaining st.

Weave in ends and wet block to set sts.

FRINGE

Cut 8in (20cm) lengths of remaining yarn. Using eight strands of yarn per tassel, fold in half and pull top of folded loop through bottom edge below last worked brp st, using a crochet hook. Take all ends through loop to make a lark's head knot and pull to tighten tassel in place. Repeat until all bottom edge brp sts have fringe attached.

ONE-COLOR BRIOCHE HAT

This is a great introduction to one-color brioche. It is the same stylish slouch hat as the two-color First Brioche Hat and also utilizes brioche decreasing in the crown shaping, making it a great step forward into the next level of skills while remaining very beginner friendly.

MATERIALS

- 215yd (197m) DK weight yarn *(Sample: West Wool, Tandem in Tangerine)*
- US 4 (3.5mm), 16in (40cm) circular needles
- US 4 (3.5mm) double-pointed needles (DPNs)
- 1 stitch marker

GAUGE (TENSION)

23 sts x 21 rows = 4in (10cm) in one-color brioche stitch on US 4 (3.5mm) needles, or size needed to obtain gauge.

MEASUREMENTS

9in (23cm) height x 19in (48cm) circumference

The hat is super stretchy, will fit up a 22–25in (56–63.5cm) head comfortably.

ABBREVIATIONS

brk	Brioche knit: knit slipped stitch together with its yarn over
brLsl	A 2-stitch decrease that slants to the left, involving three stitches: slip the first stitch knitwise, brk the following two stitches together, pass the slipped stitch over
brp	Brioche purl: purl slipped stitch together with its yarn over
CO	Cast on using the knit on method
k	Knit stitch
k2tog	Knit 2 stitches together
p	Purl stitch
PM	Place marker
sl1yo	With yarn in front, slip 1 stitch purlwise, yarn over

INSTRUCTIONS

Using US 4 (3.5mm) circular needles, CO 112 sts.

Being careful not to twist sts, PM and join in the round

Rounds 1 to 18: *P1, k1; repeat from * to end of round.

Round 19: *Sl1yo, k1; repeat from * to end of round.

Round 20: *Brp, sl1yo; repeat from * to end of round.

Round 21: *Sl1yo, brk; repeat from * to end of round.

Round 22: *Brp, sl1yo; repeat from * to end of round.

Repeat Rounds 21 and 22 until work measures 7½in (19cm) from cast-on edge.

BEGIN DECREASE SHAPING:

(Switching to DPNs when necessary)

Round 23: *Sl1yo, brLsl, [sl1yo, brk] 5 times; repeat from * to end of round. (96 sts)

Round 24: *Brp, sl1yo; repeat from * to end of round.

Round 25: *Sl1yo, brk; repeat from * to end of round.

Round 26: *Brp, sl1yo; repeat from * to end of round.

Round 27: *Sl1yo, brLsl, [sl1yo, brk] 4 times; repeat from * to end of round. (80 sts)

Round 28: *Brp, sl1yo; repeat from * to end of round.

Round 29: *Sl1yo, brk; repeat from * to end of round.

Round 30: *Brp, sl1yo; repeat from * to end of round.

Round 31: *Sl1yo, brLsl, [sl1yo, brk] 3 times; repeat from * to end of round. (64 sts)

Round 32: *Brp, sl1yo; repeat from * to end of round.

Round 33: *Sl1yo, brk; repeat from * to end of round.

Round 34: *Brp, sl1yo; repeat from * to end of round.

Round 35: *Sl1yo, brLsl, [sl1yo, brk] twice; repeat from * to end of round. (48 sts)

Round 36: *Brp, sl1yo; repeat from * to end of round.

Round 37: *Sl1yo, brk; repeat from * to end of round.

Round 38: *Brp, sl1yo; repeat from * to end of round.

Round 39: *Sl1yo, brLsl, sl1yo, brk; repeat from * to end of round. (32 sts)

Round 40: *Brp, sl1yo; repeat from * to end of round.

Round 41: *Sl1yo, brk; repeat from * to end of round.

Round 42: *Brp, sl1yo; repeat from * to end of round.

Round 43: *Sl1yo, brLsl; repeat from * to end of round. (16 sts)

Round 44: *Brp, sl1yo; repeat from * to end of round.

Round 45: *P1, brk; repeat from * to end of round.

Round 46: *K2tog; repeat from * to end of round. (8 sts)

Cut tail, draw through remaining sts to fasten off.

Weave in ends and wet block to set sts.

SPLIT MITTENS

IIIIIIIIIIIIIII

These mittens are both irresistibly fun to knit and wear! They are designed using both two-color brioche and garter stitch to create a fun, split, geometric pattern with super easy marked increases for the thumb gusset.

MATERIALS

- Color A: 88–110yd (81–101m) DK weight yarn *(Sample: West Wool, Tandem in Unicorn)*
- Color B: 98–120yd (90–110m) DK weight yarn *(Sample: West Wool, Tandem in Mariniere)*
- US 2.5 (3mm), 32in (80cm) circular needles or double-pointed needles (DPNs)
- Stitch holder or waste yarn

GAUGE (TENSION)

18 sts x 28 rows = 4in (10cm) in brioche stitch on US 2.5 (3mm) needles, or size needed to obtain gauge.

SIZES

S/M: 11in (28cm) tall x 7in (18cm) around

L/XL: 12in (30.5cm) tall x 8in (20.5cm) around

ABBREVIATIONS

brk	Brioche knit: knit slipped stitch together with its yarn over
brLsl	A 2-stitch decrease that slants to the left, involving three stitches: slip the first stitch knitwise, brk the following two stitches together, pass the slipped stitch over
brp	Brioche purl: purl slipped stitch together with its yarn over
brRsl	A 2-stitch decrease that slants to the right, involving three stitches: slip the first stitch knitwise, knit the next stitch, pass the slipped stitch over, place stitch on left hand needle and pass the following stitch over. Place stitch back on right hand needle
CO	Cast on using the knit on method
k	Knit stitch
kfb	knit into the front and back of the stitch
k2tog	Knit 2 stitches together.
p	Purl stitch
PM / SM	Place marker / slide marker
sl1yo	With yarn in front, slip 1 stitch purlwise, yarn over

INSTRUCTIONS

Using US 2.5 (3mm) needles and Color B, CO 34 (38) sts, divide stitches evenly.

Being careful not to twist sts, join in the round.

Round 1 (Color B): P15 (17), PM, p to end of round.

Round 2 (Color A): K1, *sl1yo, k1; repeat from * to marker, SM, k to end of round.

Round 2 (Color B): Sl1yo, *brp, sl1yo; repeat from * to marker, SM, p to end of round.

Round 3 (Color A): Brk, *sl1yo, brk; repeat from * to marker, SM, k to end of round.

Round 3 (Color B): Sl1yo, *brp, sl1yo; repeat from * to marker, SM, p to end of round.

Repeat Round 3 until work measures 4 (4½in) / 10 (11.5cm) from cast-on edge.

BEGIN THUMB GUSSET:

Round 4 (Color A): Brk, *sl1yo, brk; repeat from * to marker, SM, k8 (9), PM, kfb, k1, kfb, PM, k8 (9). (36, 40 sts)

Round 4 (Color B): Sl1yo, *brp, sl1yo; repeat from * to marker, SM, p to end of round (SM as you come to them).

Round 5 (Color A): Brk, *sl1yo, brk; repeat from * to marker, SM, k to end of round (SM as you come to them).

Round 5 (Color B): Sl1yo, *brp, sl1yo; repeat from * to marker, SM, p to end of round (SM as you come to them).

Round 6 (Color A): Brk, *sl1yo, brk; repeat from * to marker, SM, k8 (9), SM, kfb, k to 1 st before marker, kfb, SM, k to end of round. (38, 42 sts)

Round 6 (Color B): Sl1yo, *brp, sl1yo; repeat from * to marker, SM, p to end of round (SM as you come to them).

Round 7 (Color A): Brk, *sl1yo, brk; repeat from * to marker, SM, k to end of round (SM as you come to them).

Round 7 (Color B): Sl1yo, *brp, sl1yo; repeat from * to marker, SM, p to end of round (SM as you come to them)

Repeat Rounds 6 and 7 five (six) more times. (48, 54 sts)

Round 8 (Color A): Brk, *sl1yo, brk; repeat from * to marker, SM, k to marker, CO 3 sts, remove marker, sl17 (19) sts onto st holder or waste yarn, remove marker, k to end of round. (34, 38 sts)

Round 8 (Color B): Sl1yo, *brp, sl1yo; repeat from * to marker, SM, p to end of round.

Round 9 (Color A): Brk, *sl1yo, brk; repeat from * to marker, SM, k to end of round.

Round 9 (Color B): Sl1yo, *brp, sl1yo; repeat from * to marker, SM, p to end of round.

Repeat Round 9 until work measures 3–4in (7.5–10cm), or about 1in (2.5cm) shorter than length to finger tips.

BEGIN SHAPING (S/M SIZE):

Round 10 (Color A): Brk, *sl1yo, brk; repeat from * to marker, SM, k7, k2tog, k1, k2tog, k7. (32 sts)

Round 10 (Color B): Sl1yo, *brp, sl1yo; repeat from * to marker, SM, p to end of round.

Round 11 (Color A): Brk, *sl1yo, brk; repeat from * to marker, SM, k6, k2tog, k1, k2tog, k6. (30 sts)

Round 11 (Color B): Sl1yo, *brp, sl1yo; repeat from * to marker, SM, p to end of round.

Round 12 (Color A): [Brk, sl1yo] twice, brLsl, sl1yo, brRsl, [sl1yo, brk] twice, SM, k to end of round. (26 sts)

Round 12 (Color B): Sl1yo, *brp, sl1yo; repeat from * to marker, SM, p to end of round.

Round 13 (Color A): Brk, *sl1yo, brk; repeat from * to marker, SM, k5, k2tog, k1, k2tog, k5. (24 sts)

Round 13 (Color B): Sl1yo, *brp, sl1yo; repeat from * to marker, SM, p to end of round.

Round 14 (Color A): Brk, *sl1yo, brk; repeat from * to marker, SM, k4, k2tog, k1, k2tog, k4. (22 sts)

Round 14 (Color B): Sl1yo, *brp, sl1yo; repeat from * to marker, SM, p to end of round.

Round 15 (Color A): Brk, sl1yo, brLsl, sl1yo, brRsl, sl1yo, brk, SM, k to end of round. (18 sts)

Round 15 (Color B): Sl1yo, *brp, sl1yo; repeat from * to marker, SM, p to end of round.

Round 16 (Color A): Brk, *sl1yo, brk; repeat from * to marker, SM, k3, k2tog, k1, k2tog, k3. (16 sts)

Round 16 (Color B): Sl1yo, *brp, sl1yo; repeat from * to marker, SM, p to end of round.

Round 17 (Color A): Brk, *sl1yo, brk; repeat from * to marker, SM, k2, k2tog, k1, k2tog, k2. (14 sts)

Round 17 (Color B): Sl1yo, *brp, sl1yo; repeat from * to marker, SM, p to end of round.

Round 18 (Color A): BrLsl, sl1yo, brRsl, SM, k1, k2tog, k1, k2tog, k1. (8 sts)

Round 18 (Color B): Sl1yo, *brp, sl1yo; repeat from * to marker, SM, p to end of round.

Round 19 (Color A): Brk, *sl1yo, brk; repeat from * to marker, SM, k2tog, k1, k2tog. (6 sts)

Round 19 (Color B): K1, brp, k1, remove marker, p to end of round.

Cut tail, draw through remaining sts and fasten off.

BEGIN SHAPING (L/XL SIZE):

Round 10 (Color A): Brk, *sl1yo, brk; repeat from * to marker, SM, k8, k2tog, k1, k2tog, k8. (36 sts)

Round 10 (Color B): Sl1yo, *brp, sl1yo; repeat from * to marker, SM, p to end of round.

Round 11 (Color A): Brk, *sl1yo, brk; repeat from * to marker, SM, k7, k2tog, k1, k2tog, k7. (34 sts)

Round 11 (Color B): Sl1yo, *brp, sl1yo; repeat from * to marker, SM, p to end of round.

Round 12 (Color A): [Brk, sl1yo] twice, brLsl, sl1yo, brk, sl1yo, brRsl, [sl1yo, brk] twice, SM, k to end of round. (30 sts)

Round 12 (Color B): Sl1yo, *brp, sl1yo; repeat from * to marker, SM, p to end of round.

Round 13 (Color A): Brk, *sl1yo, brk; repeat from * to marker, SM, k6, k2tog, k1, k2tog, k6. (28 sts)

Round 13 (Color B): Sl1yo, *brp, sl1yo; repeat from * to marker, SM, p to end of round.

Round 14 (Color A): Brk, *sl1yo, brk; repeat from * to marker, SM, k5, k2tog, k1, k2tog, k5. (26 sts)

Round 14 (Color B): Sl1yo, *brp, sl1yo; repeat from * to marker, SM, p to end of round.

Round 15 (Color A): Brk, sl1yo, brLsl, sl1yo, brk, sl1yo, brRsl, sl1yo, brk, SM, k to end of round. (22 sts)

Round 15 (Color B): Sl1yo, *brp, sl1yo; repeat from * to marker, SM, p to end of round.

Round 16 (Color A): Brk, *sl1yo, brk; repeat from * to marker, SM, k4, k2tog, k1, k2tog, k4. (20 sts)

Round 16 (Color B): Sl1yo, *brp, sl1yo; repeat from * to marker, SM, p to end of round.

Round 17 (Color A): Brk, *sl1yo, brk; repeat from * to marker, SM, k3, k2tog, k1, k2tog, k3. (18 sts)

Round 17 (Color B): Sl1yo, *brp, sl1yo; repeat from * to marker, SM, p to end of round.

Round 18 (Color A): BrLsl, sl1yo, brk, sl1yo, brRsl, SM, k to end of round. (14 sts)

Round 18 (Color B): Sl1yo, *brp, sl1yo; repeat from * to marker, SM, p to end of round.

Round 19 (Color A): Brk, *sl1yo, brk; repeat from * to marker, SM, k2, k2tog, k1, k2tog, k2. (12 sts)

Round 19 (Color B): Sl1yo, *brp, sl1yo; repeat from * to marker, SM, p to end of round.

Round 20 (Color A): Brk, *sl1yo, brk; repeat from * to marker, SM, k1, k2tog, k1, k2tog, k1. (10 sts)

Round 20 (Color B): Sl1yo, *brp, sl1yo; repeat from * to marker, SM, p to end of round.

Round 21 (Color A): Sl1, k1, psso, brk, k1, sl last worked st back onto left-hand needle, pass following sl1yo st over top, slide st back to right-hand needle, remove marker, k2tog, k1, k2tog. (6 sts)

Cut tail, draw through remaining sts and fasten off.

THUMB (ALL SIZES):

Round 1 (Color A): Slide live thumb sts on needle, pick up and k 2 sts from gap, k17 (19), pick up and k 1 st from gap. (20, 22 sts)

Round 1 (Color B): P to end of round.

Round 2 (Color A): K to end of round.

Round 2 (Color B): P to end of round.

Round 3 (Color A): K2tog, k to last 2 sts, k2tog. (18, 20 sts)

Round 3 (Color B): P to end of round.

Round 4 (Color A): K2tog, k to last 2 sts, k2tog. (16, 18 sts)

Round 4 (Color B): P to end of round.

Round 5 (Color A): K2tog, k to last 2 sts, k2tog. (14, 16 sts)

Round 5 (Color B): P to end of round.

Round 6 (Color A): K to end of round.

Round 6 (Color B): P to end of round.

Repeat Round 6 until you are ½in (1cm) from thumb end (approx 1–1½in/2.5–4cm).

Round 7 (Color A): K2tog, k5 (6), k2tog, k to end of round. (12, 14 sts)

Round 7 (Color B): P to end of round.

Round 8 (Color A): K2tog, k4 (5), k2tog, k to end of round. (10, 12 sts)

Round 8 (Color B): P to end of round.

Round 9 (Color A): K2tog, k3 (4), k2tog, k to end of round. (8, 10 sts)

Round 9 (Color B): P to end of round.

LARGE SIZE ONLY:

Round 10 (Color A): K2tog, k3, k2tog, k to end of round. (8 sts)

Round 10 (Color B): P to end of round.

Break Color A, draw through remaining sts and fasten off with Color B.

Weave in ends and wet block to set sts.

RAILROAD WRAP

This wrap is another great unisex design that uses both the two-color brioche and two-color garter stitch. The simple repeat is easy to memorize and the length is customizable.

MATERIALS

- Color A: 273yd (250m) DK weight yarn
  (Sample: Manos Del Uruguay, Marla in Panna)
- Color B: 273yd (250m) DK weight yarn
  (Sample: Manos Del Uruguay, Sami in Khol)
- US 4 (3.5 mm), 32in (80cm) circular needles

GAUGE (TENSION)

19 sts x 24 rows = 4in (10cm) in two-color brioche stitch on US 4 (3.5mm) needles, or size needed to obtain gauge, after blocking.

MEASUREMENTS

74in (188cm) long x 10in (25cm) wide

NOTE

When knitting brioche flat, remember it takes two passes to equal a row. To be more specific, on a RS row you will work the first pass [brk] in Color A, then slide the stitches up to work the second pass [brp] in Color B, completing one RS row. You'll know you have finished both passes of a row when the A/B yarns are on the right needle ready to be turned for the WS row. You'll repeat this for the WS row with stitches reversed, Color A [brp] and Color B [brk], turning to work RS after both passes are complete.

ABBREVIATIONS

brk	Brioche knit: knit slipped stitch together with its yarn over
brp	Brioche purl: purl slipped stitch together with its yarn over
CO	Cast on using the knit on method
k	Knit stitch
p	Purl stitch
sl1yo	With yarn in front, slip 1 stitch purlwise, yarn over

INSTRUCTIONS

Using US 4 (3.5mm) needles and Color A, CO 53 sts.

Row 1: K to end of row.

Row 2 (RS Color A): K8, *[k1, sl1yo] 3 times, k1, k8; rep from * to end of row.

Row 2 (RS Color B): P8, *[sl1yo, brp] 3 times, sl1yo, p8; rep from * to end of row.

Row 3 (WS Color A): P8, *[brp, sl1yo] 3 times, brp, p8; rep from * to end of row.

Row 3 (WS Color B): K8, *[sl1yo, brk] 3 times, sl1yo, k8; rep from * to end of row.

Row 4 (RS Color A): K8, *[brk, sl1yo] 3 times, brk, k8; rep from * to end of row.

Row 4 (RS Color B): P8, *[sl1yo, brp] 3 times, sl1yo, p8; rep from * to end of row.

Row 5 (WS Color A): P8, *[brp, sl1yo] 3 times, brp, p8; rep from * to end of row.

Row 5 (WS Color B): K8, *[sl1yo, brk] 3 times, sl1yo, k8; rep from * to end of row.

Rep Rows 4 and 5 to desired length.

Bind (cast) off loosely.

Weave in ends and wet block to set sts.

OPEN BOOK PONCHO

This capelet style poncho was worked using a combination of two-color brioche and two-color garter stitch. The heavy bulky (chunky) yarn works up fast and makes this a very warm layering piece. There are notes included for customizing the length and width; just remember to get extra yardage if you plan on making it bigger!

MATERIALS

- Color A: 270yd (247m) heavy bulky (chunky) weight yarn *(Sample: Malabrigo, Noventa in Polar Morn)*
- Color B: 270yd (247m) heavy bulky (chunky) weight yarn *(Sample: Malabrigo, Noventa in Under The Sea)*
- US 11 (8mm), 16in (40cm) and 48in (120cm) circular needles
- US 11 (8mm) double-pointed needles (DPNs)
- 5 stitch markers

GAUGE (TENSION)

8 sts x 13 rows = 4in (10cm) in two-color brioche stitch on US 11 (8mm) needles, or size needed to obtain gauge, after blocking.

MEASUREMENTS

80in (203cm) around, 17in (43cm) deep, 11in (28cm) neck opening

Size is customizable.

NOTE

This project uses a yarn over bind (cast) off for a stretchy edge – see step-by-step instructions for how to work this in the General Techniques section.

ABBREVIATIONS

brk	Brioche knit: knit slipped stitch together with its yarn over
brkyobrk	A 2-stitch increase in brioche knit: brioche knit, yarn over, brioche knit into the same stitch
brp	Brioche purl: purl slipped stitch together with its yarn over
k	Knit stitch
kfb	Knit into the front and back of the stitch
p	Purl stitch
PM / SM	Place marker / slide marker
sl1yo	With yarn in front, slip 1 stitch purlwise, yarn over

INSTRUCTIONS

Using US 11 (8mm) circular needles and Color A, CO 52 sts.

Being careful not to twist sts, PM and join in the round.

Rounds 1 to 3: *P1, k1; repeat from * to end of round.

Round 4 (Color A): [Sl1yo, k1] 6 times, PM, k1, PM, k1, [sl1yo, k1] twice, PM, k1, PM, k1, *sl1yo, k1, rep from * to end of round.

Round 4 (Color B): *Brp, sl1yo; repeat from * to marker, SM, p1, SM, sl1yo, **brp, sl1yo; repeat from ** to marker, SM, p1, SM, sl1yo, ***brp, sl1yo; rep from *** to end of round.

Round 5 (Color A): *Sl1yo, brk; repeat from * to marker, SM, kfb, SM, brk, **sl1yo, brk; repeat from ** to marker, SM, kfb, SM, brk, ***sl1yo, brk; rep from *** to end of round. (54 sts)

Round 5 (Color B): *Brp, sl1yo; repeat from * to marker, SM, p2, SM, sl1yo, **brp, sl1yo; repeat from ** to marker, SM, p2, SM, sl1yo, ***brp, sl1yo; rep from *** to end of round.

Round 6 (Color A): *Sl1yo, brk; repeat from * to 2 sts before marker, sl1yo, brkyobrk, SM, k to marker, SM, brkyobrk, **sl1yo, brk; repeat from ** to 2 sts before marker, sl1yo, brkyobrk, SM, k to marker, SM, brkyobrk, ***sl1yo, brk; rep from *** to end of round. (62 sts)

Round 6 (Color B): *Brp, sl1yo; repeat from * to 2 sts before marker, p1, sl1yo, SM, p to marker, SM, sl1yo, p1, sl1yo, **brp, sl1yo; repeat from ** to 2 sts before marker, p1, sl1yo, SM, p to marker, SM, sl1yo, p1, sl1yo, ***brp, sl1yo; rep from *** to end of round.

Round 7 (Color A): *Sl1yo, brk; repeat from * to marker, SM, k to marker, SM, brk, **sl1yo, brk; repeat from ** to marker, SM, k to marker, SM, brk, ***sl1yo, brk; rep from *** to end of round.

Round 7 (Color B): *Brp, sl1yo; repeat from * to marker, SM, p to marker, SM, sl1yo, **brp, sl1yo; repeat from ** to marker, SM, p to marker, SM, sl1yo, ***brp, sl1yo; rep from *** to end of round.

Round 8 (Color A): *Sl1yo, brk; repeat from * to marker, SM, kfb, k to 1 st before marker, kfb, SM, brk, **sl1yo, brk; repeat from ** to marker, SM, kfb, k to 1 st before marker, kfb, SM, brk, ***sl1yo, brk, rep from *** to end of round. (66 sts)

Round 8 (Color B): *Brp, sl1yo; repeat from * to marker, SM, p to marker, SM, sl1yo, **brp, sl1yo; repeat from ** to marker, SM, p to marker, SM, sl1yo, ***brp, sl1yo; rep from *** to end of round.

Repeat Rounds 6 to 8 six more times. (138 sts)

Round 27 (Color A): *Sl1yo, brk; repeat from * to marker, SM, k to marker, SM, brk, **sl1yo, brk; repeat from ** to marker, SM, k to marker, SM, brk, ***sl1yo, brk; rep from *** to end of round.

Round 27 (Color B): *Brp, sl1yo; repeat from * to marker, SM, p to marker, SM, sl1yo, **brp, sl1yo; repeat from ** to marker, SM, p to marker, SM, sl1yo, ***brp, sl1yo; rep from *** to end of round.

Round 28 (Color A): *Sl1yo, brk; repeat from * to marker, SM, k to marker, SM, brk, **sl1yo, brk; repeat from ** to marker, SM, k to marker, SM, brk, ***sl1yo, brk; rep from *** to end of round.

Round 28 (Color B): *Brp, sl1yo; repeat from * to marker, SM, p to marker, SM, sl1yo, **brp, sl1yo; repeat from ** to marker, SM, p to marker, SM, sl1yo, ***brp, sl1yo; rep from *** to end of round.

Round 29 (Color A): *Sl1yo, brk; repeat from * to marker, SM, kfb, k to 1 st before marker, kfb, SM, brk, **sl1yo, brk; repeat from ** to marker, SM, kfb, k to 1 st before marker, kfb, SM, brk, ***sl1yo, brk; rep from *** to end of round. (142 sts)

Round 29 (Color B): *Brp, sl1yo; repeat from * to marker, SM, p to marker, SM, sl1yo, **brp, sl1yo; repeat from ** to marker, SM, p to marker, SM, sl1yo, ***brp, sl1yo; rep from *** to end of round.

Repeat Rounds 28 and 29 seven more times. (170 sts)

NOTE: To make this pattern both longer and wider repeat Rounds 28 and 29; four completed rounds equals an additional 1in (2.5cm) in length and 1½in (4cm) in width. Remember to buy extra yarn if you will be making it bigger!

Break Color B.

Round 44 (Color A): *K1, brk; repeat from * to marker, remove marker, k to marker, remove marker, brk, **k1, brk; repeat from ** to marker, remove marker, k to marker, remove marker, brk, ***k1, brk; rep from *** to end of round.

Using Color A bind (cast) off as follows: K1, *yo purlwise, k1, pass yo and k st over last k st; repeat from * to end of row, cut yarn and draw through remaining st.

Weave in ends, wet block to set sts.

SOL REVIVAL SHAWL

This crescent shawl is a total texture party on the needles. It's made using two-color brioche and garter stitch and then adds some fun colorful bobble stitches in the mix. The final shawl is big, luxurious, with fun color pops, and the DK weight is sure to keep you warm.

MATERIALS

- Color A: 400yd (366m) DK weight yarn *(Sample: West Wool, Tandem in Pebble)*
- Color B: 365yd (334m) DK weight yarn *(Sample: West Wool, Tandem in Mouse)*
- Color C: 145yd (133m) DK weight yarn *(Sample: West Wool, Tandem in Unicorn)*
- Color D: 135yd (124m) DK weight yarn *(Sample: West Wool, Tandem in Sherbert)*
- US 6 (4mm), 40in (100cm) circular needles
- 2 stitch markers

GAUGE (TENSION)

10 sts x 24 rows = 4in in two-color brioche stitch on US 6 (4mm) needles, or size needed to obtain gauge.

MEASUREMENTS

109in (277cm) wingspan, 19in (48cm) long

NOTE

When knitting brioche flat, remember it takes two passes to equal a row. To be more specific, on a RS row you will work the first pass [brk] in Color A, then slide the stitches up to work the second pass [brp] in Color B, completing one RS row. You'll know you have finished both passes of a row when the A/B yarns are on the right needle ready to be turned for the WS row. You'll repeat this for the WS row with stitches reversed, Color A [brp] and Color B [brk], turning to work RS after both passes are complete.

ABBREVIATIONS

brk	Brioche knit: knit slipped stitch together with its yarn over
brp	Brioche purl: purl slipped stitch together with its yarn over
CO	Cast on using the knit on method
k	Knit stitch
kyok	Knit, yarn over, knit into the same stitch
kyokyok	A 4-stitch increase: knit, yarn over, knit, yarn over, knit into the same stitch
k3tog	Knit 3 stitches together
p	Purl stitch
pfb	Purl into front and back of stitch
PM / SM	Place marker / slide marker
psso	Pass slipped stitch(es) over
sl	Slip number of stitches stated purlwise
sl1yo	With yarn in front, slip 1 stitch purlwise, yarn over
wyib / wyif	With yarn in back / with yarn in front.

INSTRUCTIONS

Using US 6 (4mm) needles and Color A, CO 9 sts.

Row 1 (WS Color A): Pfb, p7, pfb. (11 sts)

Row 1 (WS Color B): K to end of row.

Row 2 (RS Color A): K1, kyok, k to last 2 sts, kyok, k1. (15 sts)

Row 2 (RS Color B): P to end of row.

Row 3 (WS Color A): Pfb, p to last st, pfb. (17 sts)

Row 3 (WS Color B): K to end of row.

Row 4 (RS Color A): K1, kyok, k to last 2 sts, kyok, k1. (21 sts)

Row 4 (RS Color B): P to end of row.

Row 5 (WS Color A): Pfb, PM, purl to last st, PM, pfb. (23 sts)

Row 5 (WS Color B): K to end of row, SM as you come to them.

SECTION 1

Row 6 (RS Color A): K1, kyok, SM, k1, *sl1yo, k1; repeat from * to marker, SM, kyok, k1. (27 sts)

Row 6 (RS Color B): P4, SM, sl1yo, *brp, sl1yo; repeat from * to marker, SM, p4.

Row 7 (WS Color A): Pfb, p to marker, SM, brp, *sl1yo, brp; repeat from * to marker, SM, p to last st, pfb. (29 sts)

Row 7 (WS Color B): K to marker, SM, sl1yo, *brk, sl1yo; repeat from * to marker, SM, k to end of row.

Row 8 (RS Color A): K1, kyok, k to marker, SM, brk, *sl1yo, brk; repeat from * to marker, SM, k to last 2 sts, kyok, k1. (33 sts)

Row 8 (RS Color B): P to marker, SM, sl1yo, *brp, sl1yo; repeat from * to marker, SM, p to end of row.

Repeat Rows 7 and 8 twice more. (45 sts)

Break Color B.

Row 13 (WS Color A): Pfb, p to marker, remove marker, brp, *p1, brp; repeat from * to marker, remove marker, purl to last st, pfb. (47 sts)

Row 14 (RS Color C): K1, kyok, kyokyok, *sl1 wyib, kyokyok; repeat from * to last 2 sts, kyok, k1. (139 sts)

Row 15 (WS Color C): Sl1, k3, *p5, sl1 wyif; repeat from * to last 9 sts, p5, k3, sl1, break Color C.

Row 16 (RS Color A): K1, kyok, PM, k2, sl2, k3tog, psso, *k1, sl2, k3tog, psso; repeat from * to last 4 sts, k2, PM, kyok, k1. (55 sts)

Slide sts back to work RS.

SECTION 2

Row 17 (RS Color B): P to marker, SM, sl1yo, *p1, sl1yo; repeat from * to marker, SM, p to end of row.

Row 18 (WS Color A): Pfb, p to marker, SM, brp, *sl1yo, brp; repeat from * to marker, SM, p to last st, pfb. (57 sts)

Row 18 (WS Color B): K to marker, SM, sl1yo, *brk, sl1yo; repeat from * to marker, SM, k to end of row.

Row 19 (RS Color A): K1, kyok, k to marker, SM, brk, *sl1yo, brk; repeat from * to marker, SM, k to last 2 sts, kyok, k1. (61 sts)

Row 19 (RS Color B): P to marker, SM, sl1yo, *brp, sl1yo; repeat from * to marker, SM, p to end of row.

Repeat Rows 18 and 19 twice more. (73 sts)

Break Color B.

Row 24 (WS Color A): Pfb, p to marker, remove marker, brp, *p1, brp; repeat from * to marker, remove marker, p to last st, pfb. (75 sts)

Row 25 (RS Color D): K1, kyok, kyokyok, *sl1 wyib, kyokyok; repeat from * to last 2 sts, kyok, k1. (223 sts)

Row 26 (WS Color D): Sl1, k3, *p5, sl1 wyif; repeat from * to last 9 sts, p5, k3, sl1, break Color D.

Row 27 (RS Color A): K1, kyok, PM, k2, sl2, k3tog, psso, *k1, sl2, k3tog, psso; repeat from * to last 4 sts, k2, PM, kyok, k1. (83 sts)

Slide sts back to work RS.

SECTION 3

Row 28 (RS Color B): P to marker, SM, sl1yo, *p1, sl1yo; repeat from * to marker, SM, p to end of row.

Row 29 (WS Color A): Pfb, p to marker, SM, brp, *sl1yo, brp; repeat from * to marker, SM, p to last st, pfb. (85 sts)

Row 29 (WS Color B): K to marker, SM, sl1yo, *brk, sl1yo; repeat from * to marker, SM, k to end of row.

Row 30 (RS Color A): K1, kyok, k to marker, SM, brk, *sl1yo, brk; repeat from * to marker, SM, k to last 2 sts, kyok, k1. (89 sts)

Row 30 (RS Color B): P to marker, SM, sl1yo, *brp, sl1yo; repeat from * to marker, SM, p to end of row.

Repeat Rows 29 and 30 twice more. (101 sts)

Break Color B.

Row 35 (WS Color A): Pfb, p to marker, remove marker, brp, *p1, brp; repeat from * to marker, remove marker, p to last st, pfb. (103 sts)

Row 36 (RS Color C): K1, kyok, kyokyok, *sl1 wyib, kyokyok; repeat from * to last 2 sts, kyok, k1. (307 sts)

Row 37 (WS Color C): Sl1, k3, *p5, sl1 wyif; repeat from * to last 9 sts, p5, k3, sl1, break Color C.

Row 38 (RS Color A): K1, kyok, PM, k2, sl2, k3tog, psso, *k1, sl2, k3tog, psso; repeat from * to last 4 sts, k2, PM, kyok, k1. (111 sts)

Slide sts back to work RS.

SECTION 4

Row 39 (RS Color B): P to marker, SM, sl1yo, *p1, sl1yo; repeat from * to marker, SM, p to end of row.

Row 40 (WS Color A): Pfb, p to marker, SM, brp, *sl1yo, brp; repeat from * to marker, SM, p to last st, pfb. (113 sts)

Row 40 (WS Color B): K to marker, SM, sl1yo, *brk, sl1yo; repeat from * to marker, SM, k to end of row.

Row 41 (RS Color A): K1, kyok, k to marker, SM, brk, *sl1yo, brk; repeat from * to marker, SM, k to last 2 sts, kyok, k1. (117 sts)

Row 41 (RS Color B): P to marker, SM, sl1yo, *brp, sl1yo; repeat from * to marker, SM, p to end of row.

Repeat Rows 40 and 41 twice more. (129 sts)

Break Color B.

Row 46 (WS Color A): Pfb, p to marker, remove marker, brp, *p1, brp; repeat from * to marker, remove marker, p to last st, pfb. (131 sts)

Row 47 (RS Color D): K1, kyok, kyokyok, *sl1 wyib, kyokyok; repeat from * to last 2 sts, kyok, k1. (391 sts)

Row 48 (WS Color D): Sl1, k3, *p5, sl1 wyif; repeat from * to last 9 sts, p5, k3, sl1, break Color D.

Row 49 (RS Color A): K1, kyok, PM, k2, sl2, k3tog, psso, *k1, sl2, k3tog, psso; repeat from * to last 4 sts, k2, PM, kyok, k1. (139 sts)

Slide sts back to work RS.

Repeat all Rows of Section 3 and Section 4 four more times. (363 sts)

Row 72 (RS Color B): P to marker, SM, sl1yo, *p1, sl1yo; repeat from * to marker, SM, p to end of row

Row 73 (WS Color A): Pfb, p to marker, SM, brp, *sl1yo, brp; repeat from * to marker, SM, p to last st, pfb. (365 sts)

Row 73 (WS Color B): K to marker, SM, sl1yo, *brk, sl1yo; repeat from * to marker, SM, k to end of row.

Row 74 (RS Color A): K1, kyok, k to marker, SM, brk, *sl1yo, brk; repeat from * to marker, SM, k to last 2 sts, kyok, k1. (369 sts)

Row 74 (RS Color B): P to marker, SM, sl1yo, *brp, sl1yo; repeat from * to marker, SM, p to end of row.

Repeat Rows 73 and 74 twice more. (381 sts)

Break Color B.

Row 79 (WS Color A): Pfb, p to marker, remove marker, brp, *p1, brp; repeat from * to marker, SM, p to last st, pfb. (383 sts)

Break color A.

With right side facing and Color C, picot bind (cast) off as follows: *Using knit on method, CO 3, bind (cast) off 6 sts, place remaining st on left-hand needle; repeat from * to last st, cut yarn and draw through remaining st.

Weave in ends and wet block to set sts.

BOOKISH HEADBAND

IIIIIIIIIIIIIII

The construction of this headband starts with a thick i-cord that eventually increases into a fun split color headband, before decreasing back into an i-cord. This style can be worn many different ways.

MATERIALS

- Color A: 80yd (73m) bulky (chunky) weight yarn *(Sample: Manos Del Uruguay, Cardo in Putty)*
- Color B: 30yd (28m) bulky (chunky) weight yarn *(Sample: Manos Del Uruguay, Cardo in Peach Blossom)*
- Color C: 30yd (28m) bulky (chunky) weight yarn *(Sample: Manos Del Uruguay, Cardo in Ethereal)*
- US 8 (5mm) double-pointed needles (DPNs)

GAUGE (TENSION)

12 sts x 14 rows = 4in (10cm) in two-color brioche stitch on US 8 (5mm) needles, or size needed to obtain gauge.

MEASUREMENTS

5in (13cm) tall x 37in (94cm) with ties

NOTE

When knitting two-color brioche flat remember that it takes two passes to equal a row. On your RS row you will work the first pass [brk] in Color A, then slide the stitches back to work the second pass [brp] in Color B, completing one RS row. You'll know you have finished both passes of a row when the A/B yarns are on the right needle ready to be turned for the WS row. You'll repeat this for the WS row with stitches reversed, Color A [brp] and Color B [brk], turning to work RS after both passes are complete.

ABBREVIATIONS

brk	Brioche knit: knit slipped stitch together with its yarn over
brkyobrk	A 2-stitch increase in brioche knit: brioche knit, yarn over, brioche knit into the same stitch
brp	Brioche purl: purl slipped stitch together with its yarn over
brRsl	A 2-stitch decrease that slants to the right, involving three stitches: slip the first stitch knitwise, knit the next stitch, pass the slipped stitch over, place stitch on left hand needle and pass the following stitch over. Place stitch back on right hand needle
CO	Cast on using the knit on method
k	Knit stitch
kyok	Knit, yarn over, knit into the same stitch
k2tog	Knit 2 stitches together
p	Purl stitch
pfb	Purl into front and back of stitch
sl1yo	With yarn in front, slip 1 stitch purlwise, yarn over

INSTRUCTIONS

Using US 8 (5mm) needles and Color A, CO 5 sts, slide sts up to start i-cord.

Row 1 (RS Color A): K to end of row, slide sts back up needle to be worked again.

Repeat Row 1 for 12in (30cm).

Row 2 (WS Color A): Pfb, p to last st, pfb. (7 sts)

Row 3 (RS Color A): K2, sl1yo, kyok, sl1yo, k2. (9 sts)

Row 3 (RS Color B): P1, sl1yo, brp, sl1yo, p1, sl1yo, brp, sl1yo, p1.

Row 4 (WS Color A): P1, brp, *sl1yo, brp; rep from * to last st, p1.

Row 4 (WS Color B): K1, sl1yo, brk, sl1yo, brkyobrk, sl1yo, brk, sl1yo, k1. (11 sts)

Row 5 (RS Color A): K1, brk, sl1yo, brk, sl1yo, k1, sl1yo, brk, sl1yo, brk, k1.

Row 5 (RS Color B): P1, sl1yo, *brp, sl1yo; rep from * to last st, p1.

Row 6 (WS Color A): P1, brp, *sl1yo, brp; rep from * to last st, p1.

Row 6 (WS Color B): K1, sl1yo, *brk, sl1yo; rep from * to last st, k1.

Row 7 (RS Color A): K1, [brk, sl1yo] twice, brkyobrk, [sl1yo, brk] twice, k1. (13 sts)

Row 7 (RS Color B): P1, [sl1yo, brp] twice, sl1yo, p1, sl1yo, [brp, sl1yo] twice, p1.

Row 8 (WS Color A): P1, brp, *sl1yo, brp; rep from * to last st, p1.

Row 8 (WS Color B): K1, [sl1yo, brk] twice, sl1yo, brkyobrk, sl1yo, [brk, sl1yo] twice, k1. (15 sts)

Row 9 (RS Color A): K1, [brk, sl1yo] 3 times, k1, [sl1yo, brk] 3 times, k1.

Row 9 (RS Color B): P1, sl1yo, *brp, sl1yo; rep from * to last st, p1.

Row 10 (WS Color A): P1, brp, *sl1yo, brp; rep from * to last st, p1.

Row 10 (WS Color B): K1, sl1yo, *brk, sl1yo; rep from * to last st, k1.

Row 11 (RS Color A): K1, [brk, sl1yo] 3 times, brkyobrk, [sl1yo, brk] 3 times, k1. (17 sts)

Row 11 (RS Color B): P1, [sl1yo, brp] 3 times, sl1yo, p1, sl1yo, [brp, sl1yo] 3 times, p1.

Row 12 (WS Color A): P1, brp, *sl1yo, brp; rep from * to last st, p1.

Row 12 (WS Color B): K1, sl1yo, *brk, sl1yo; rep from * to last st, k1.

Row 13 (RS Color A): K1, brk, *sl1yo, brk; rep from * to last st, k1.

Row 13 (RS Color B): P1, *sl1yo, brp; rep from * to last 2 sts, sl1yo, p1.

Row 14 (WS Color A): P1, brp, *sl1yo, brp; rep from * to last st, p1.

Row 14 (WS Color B): K1, sl1yo, *brk, sl1yo; rep from * to last st, k1.

Repeat Rows 13 to 14 until work measures 8in (20cm) from first brioche row.

Break Color B, join Color C.

Row 15 (RS Color A): K1, brk, *sl1yo, brk; rep from * to last st, k1.

Row 15 (RS Color C): P1, *sl1yo, brp; rep from * to last 2 sts, sl1yo, p1.

Row 16 (WS Color A): P1, brp, *sl1yo, brp; rep from * to last st, p1.

Row 16 (WS Color C): K1, sl1yo, *brk, sl1yo; rep from * to last st, k1.

Repeat Rows 15 and 16 until work measures 6in (15cm) from end of Color B.

Row 17 (RS Color A): K1, [brk, sl1yo] 3 times, brRsl, [sl1yo, brk] 3 times, k1. (15 sts)

Row 17 (RS Color C): P1, sl1yo, *brp, sl1yo; rep from * to last st, p1.

Row 18 (WS Color A): P1 , brp, *sl1yo, brp; rep from * to last st, p1.

Row 18 (WS Color C): K1, sl1yo, [brk, sl1yo] twice, brRsl, sl1yo, [brk, sl1yo] twice, k1. (13 sts)

Row 19 (RS Color A): K1, brk, *sl1yo, brk; rep from * to last st, k1.

Row 19 (RS Color C): P1, sl1yo, *brp, sl1yo; rep from * to last st, p1.

Row 20 (WS Color A): P1, brp, *sl1yo, brp; rep from * to last st, p1.

Row 20 (WS Color C): K1, sl1yo, *brk, sl1yo; rep from * to last st, k1.

Row 21 (RS Color A): K1, [brk, sl1yo] twice, brRsl, [sl1yo, brk] twice, k1. (11 sts)

Row 21 (RS Color C): P1, sl1yo, *brp, sl1yo; rep from * to last st, p1.

Row 22 (WS Color A): P1, brp, *sl1yo, brp; rep from * to last st, p1.

Row 22 (WS Color C): K1, sl1yo, brk, sl1yo, brRsl, sl1yo, brk, sl1yo, k1. (9 sts)

Row 23 (RS Color A): K1, brk, *sl1yo, brk; rep from * to last st, k1.

Row 23 (RS Color C): P1, sl1yo, *brp, sl1yo; rep from * to last st, p1.

Row 24 (WS Color A): P1, brp, *sl1yo, brp; rep from * to last st, p1

Row 24 (WS Color C): K1, sl1yo, *brk, sl1yo; rep from * to last st, k1.

Row 25 (RS Color A): K1, brk, sl1yo, brRsl, sl1yo, brk, k1. (7 sts)

Row 25 (RS Color C): P1, sl1yo, *brp, sl1yo; rep from * to last st, p1.

Break Color C.

Row 26 (WS Color A): P1, brp, *sl1yo, brp; rep from * to last st, p1.

Row 27 (RS Color A): K2tog, brp, k1, brp, k2tog. (5 sts)

Slide sts back up needle to work i-cord.

Row 28 (RS Color A): K to end of row, slide sts back up needle to be worked again.

Repeat Row 28 for 12in (30cm).

Bind (cast) off.

Weave in ends and block to measurements.

BRIOCHE SLIPPERS

These cozy slippers are knit top down in bulky (chunky) yarn with an afterthought heel. They are great for staying warm on cold days. If you are between sizes I recommend sizing down as brioche is very stretchy!

MATERIALS

- Color A: 80–150yd (73–137m) bulky (chunky) weight yarn *(Sample: Malabrigo, Chunky in Natural)*
- Color B: 80–150yd (73–137m) bulky (chunky) weight yarn *(Sample: Malabrigo, Chunky in Whole Grain)*
- Waste yarn
- US 8 (5mm) 32–40in (80–100cm) circular needles or double-pointed needles (DPNs)
- 1 stitch marker
- Darning needle

GAUGE (TENSION)

12 sts x 16 rows = 4in (10cm) in two-color brioche stitch on US 8 (5mm) needles, or size needed to obtain gauge.

SIZES

8 / 9 / 10in (20.5 / 23 / 25.5cm) foot circumference

10 /11 /12in (25.5 / 28 / 30.5cm) leg circumference

Length completely customizable.

ABBREVIATIONS

brk	Brioche knit: knit slipped stitch together with its yarn over
brp	Brioche purl: purl slipped stitch together with its yarn over
CO	Cast on using the knit on method
k	Knit stitch
k2tog	Knit 2 stitches together
k2togtbl	Knit 2 stitches together through the back loop
p	Purl stitch
PM	Place marker
sl	Slip stitch purlwise
sl1yo	With yarn in front, slip 1 stitch purlwise, yarn over

INSTRUCTIONS

Using US 8 (5mm) needles and Color A, CO 28 (32, 36) sts and divide sts evenly.

Being careful not to twist sts, PM and join in the round.

Round 1 (Color A): K to end of round.

Round 2 (Color B): *P1, sl1yo; repeat from * to end of round.

Round 3 (Color A): *Sl1yo, brk; repeat from * to end of round.

Round 3 (Color B): *Brp, sl1yo; repeat from * to end of round.

Repeat Round 3 another 22 times.

SET UP AFTERTHOUGHT HEEL:

Round 26 (Color A): [K1, brk] 7 times, *sl1yo, brk; repeat from * to end of round.

Using waste yarn, k13 (15, 17). Sl these 13 (15, 17) sts back to the right needle to be worked in Color B.

Round 26 (Color B): K13 (15, 17), sl1yo, *brp, sl1yo; repeat from * to end of round.

Round 27 (Color A): K13 (15, 17), brk, *sl1yo, brk; repeat from * to end of round.

Round 27 (Color B): K13 (15, 17), sl1yo, *brp, sl1yo; repeat from * to end of round.

Repeat Round 27 until you are 1½in (4cm) from the end of your toes.

BEGIN TOES:

Round 28 (Color B): K13 (15, 17), brk, *k1, brk; repeat from * to end of round.

Round 29 (Color B): K to end of round.

Round 30 (Color B): K1, k2togtbl, k8 (10, 12), k2tog, k2, k2togtbl, k8 (10, 12), k2tog, k1. (24, 28, 32 sts)

Round 31 (Color B): K to end of round.

Round 32 (Color B): K1, k2togtbl, k6 (8, 10), k2tog, k2, k2togtbl, k6 (8, 10), k2tog, k1. (20, 24, 28 sts)

Round 33 (Color B): K to end of round.

Round 34 (Color B): K1, k2togtbl, k4 (6, 8), k2tog, k2, k2togtbl, k4 (6, 8), k2tog, k1. (16, 20, 24 sts)

Round 35 (Color B): K to end of round.

Round 36 (Color B): K1, k2togtbl, k2 (4, 6), k2tog, k2, k2togtbl, k2 (4, 6), k2tog, k1. (12, 16, 20 sts)

Round 37 (Color B): K to end of round.

MEDIUM AND LARGE SIZE ONLY:

Round 38 (Color B): K1, k2togtbl, k2 (4), k2tog, k2, k2togtbl, k2 (4), k2tog, k1. (12, 16 sts)

Round 39 (Color B): K to end of round.

ALL SIZES:

Break yarn leaving 18in (46cm) tail. Using the kitchener st, graft remaining toe sts together.

MAKE AFTERTHOUGHT HEEL:

Remove waste yarn and place 26 (30, 34) sts back on needles, divided evenly *(see General Techniques)*.

Set up round: Pick up and k 2 sts, k across 13 (15, 17) sts, pick up and k 2 sts, k across 13 (15, 17) sts. (30, 34, 38 sts)

Round 1: [K2, k2togtbl, k7 (9, 11), k2tog, k2] twice. (26, 30, 34 sts)

Round 2: K to end of round.

Round 3: [K2, k2togtbl, k5 (7, 9), k2tog, k2] twice. (22, 26, 30 sts)

Round 4: K to end of round.

Round 5: [K2, k2togtbl, k3 (5, 7), k2tog, k2] twice. (18, 22, 26 sts)

Round 6: K to end of round.

Round 7: [K2, k2togtbl, k1 (3, 5), k2tog, k2] twice. (14, 18, 22 sts)

Round 8: K to end of round.

Using the kitchener st, graft remaining heel sts together.

Weave in ends and wet block to measurements.

GENERAL TECHNIQUES

LONG TAIL / CONTINENTAL CAST ON

This method creates an elastic edge suitable for stitches or yarns without much stretch.

1. Measure out about 1in (2.5cm) of yarn for each stitch to be made. Make a slip knot on the left-hand needle at the end of the measured yarn. Wrap the ball-end of the yarn around the index finger and the cut end around the thumb.
2. Insert the tip of the right-hand needle up through the loop on the thumb.
3. Catch the loop of yarn on the index finger and pull through the loop on the thumb.
4. Drop the loop from the thumb and pull tight to form a stitch on the needle. Repeat these steps until you have the required number of stitches.

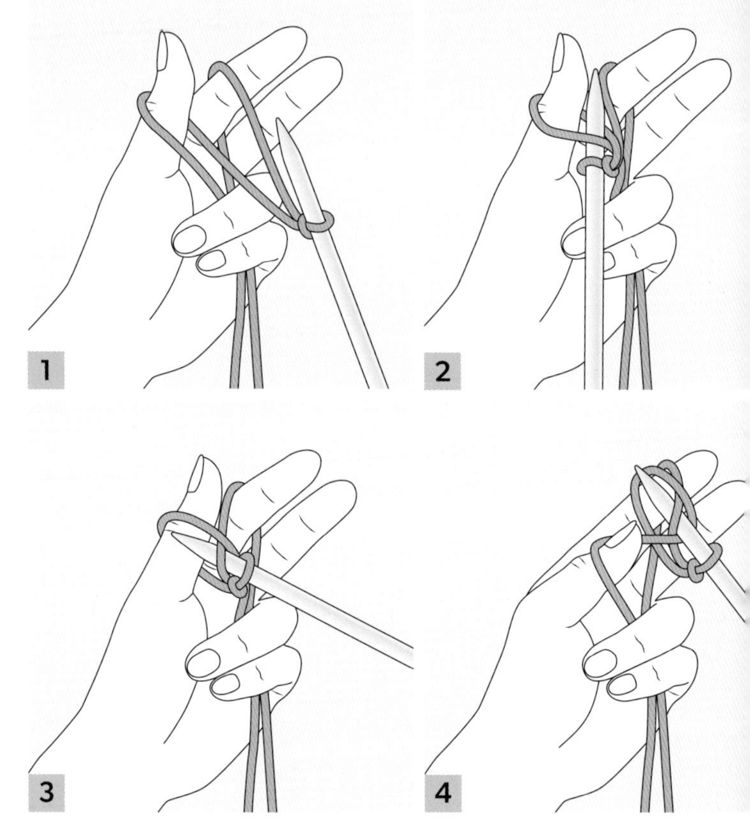

KNIT STITCH ENGLISH (K)

With the English method the yarn is held in the right hand, at the back of the work for the knit stitch.

1. Hold the needle with the stitches in your left hand, with the yarn at the back. Insert the tip of the right-hand needle into the first stitch from front to back and left to right.
2. Take the yarn under and around the right-hand needle from left to right.
3. Use the tip of the right-hand needle to pull the loop through the stitch on the left-hand needle to form a new stitch on the right-hand needle.
4. Slide off the stitch on the left-hand needle. Repeat these steps to the end of the row.

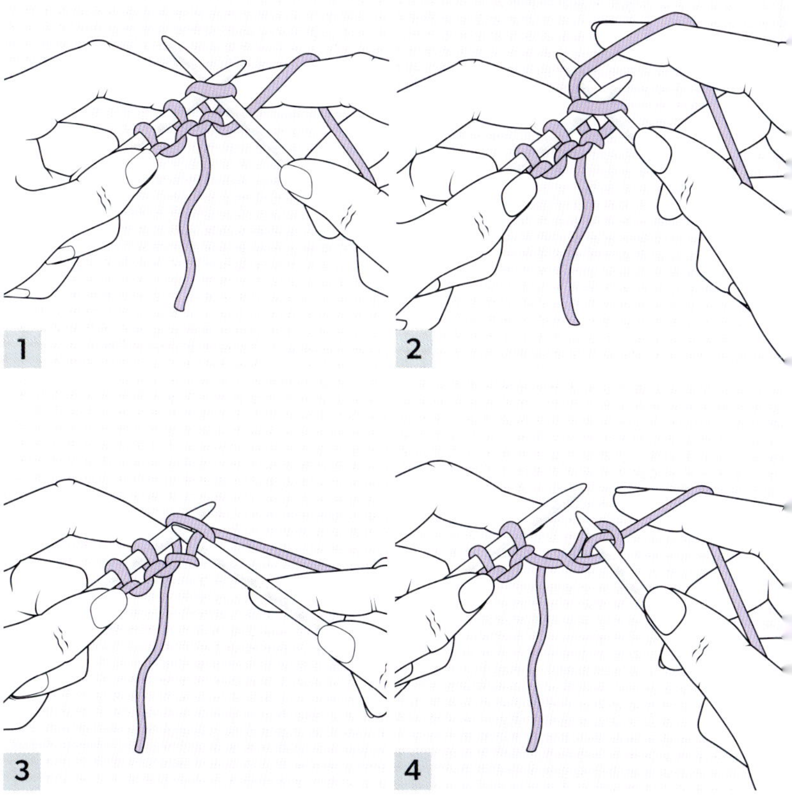

KNIT STITCH CONTINENTAL (K)

With the Continental method the yarn is wrapped around the index finger of the left hand, at the back of the work for the knit stitch.

1. Insert the tip of the right-hand needle into the first stitch from front to back and left to right.
2. Take the yarn over and around the right-hand needle from left to right.
3. Use the tip of the right-hand needle to pull the loop through the stitch on the left-hand needle to form a new stitch on the right-hand needle.
4. Slide off the stitch on the left-hand needle. Repeat these steps to the end of the row.

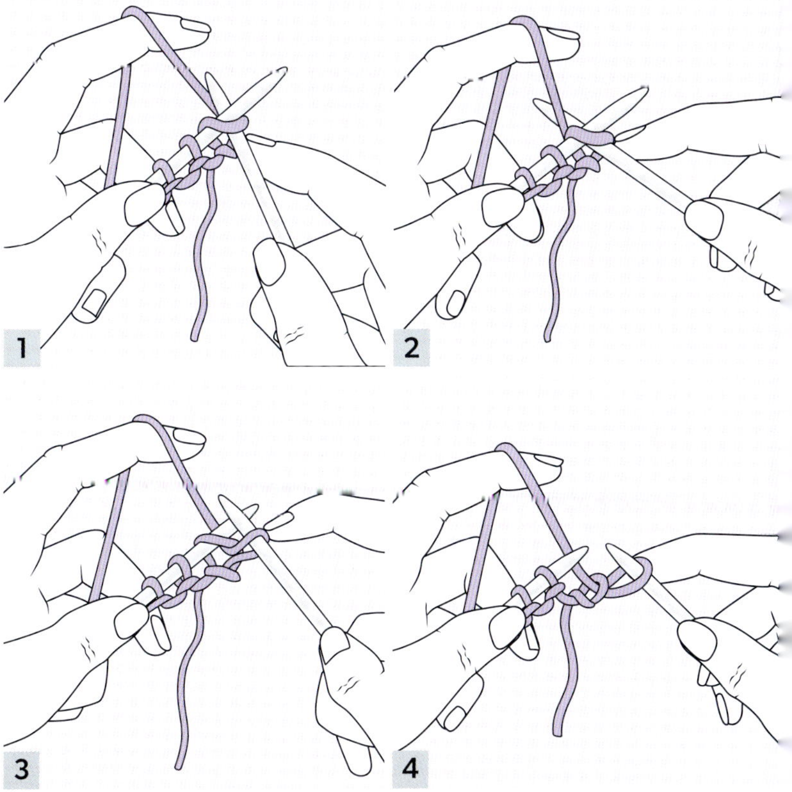

PURL STITCH ENGLISH (P)

With the English method the yarn is held in the right hand, at the front of the work for the purl stitch.

1. Hold the needle with the stitches in your left hand, with the yarn at the front. Insert the tip of the right-hand needle into the first stitch from right to left.
2. Take the yarn over and around the right-hand needle to form the next stitch.
3. Use the tip of the right-hand needle to pull the loop through the stitch on the left-hand needle to form a new stitch on the right-hand needle.
4. Slide off the stitch on the left-hand needle. Repeat these steps to the end of the row.

PURL STITCH CONTINENTAL (P)

With the Continental method the yarn is wrapped around the index finger of the left hand, at the front of the work for the purl stitch.

1. Hold the needle with the stitches in your left hand, with the yarn at the front. Insert the tip of the right-hand needle into the first stitch from right to left.
2. Take the yarn over and around the right-hand needle to form the next stitch.
3. Use the tip of the right-hand needle to pull the loop through the stitch on the left-hand needle to form a new stitch on the right-hand needle.
4. Slide off the stitch on the left-hand needle. Repeat these steps to the end of the row.

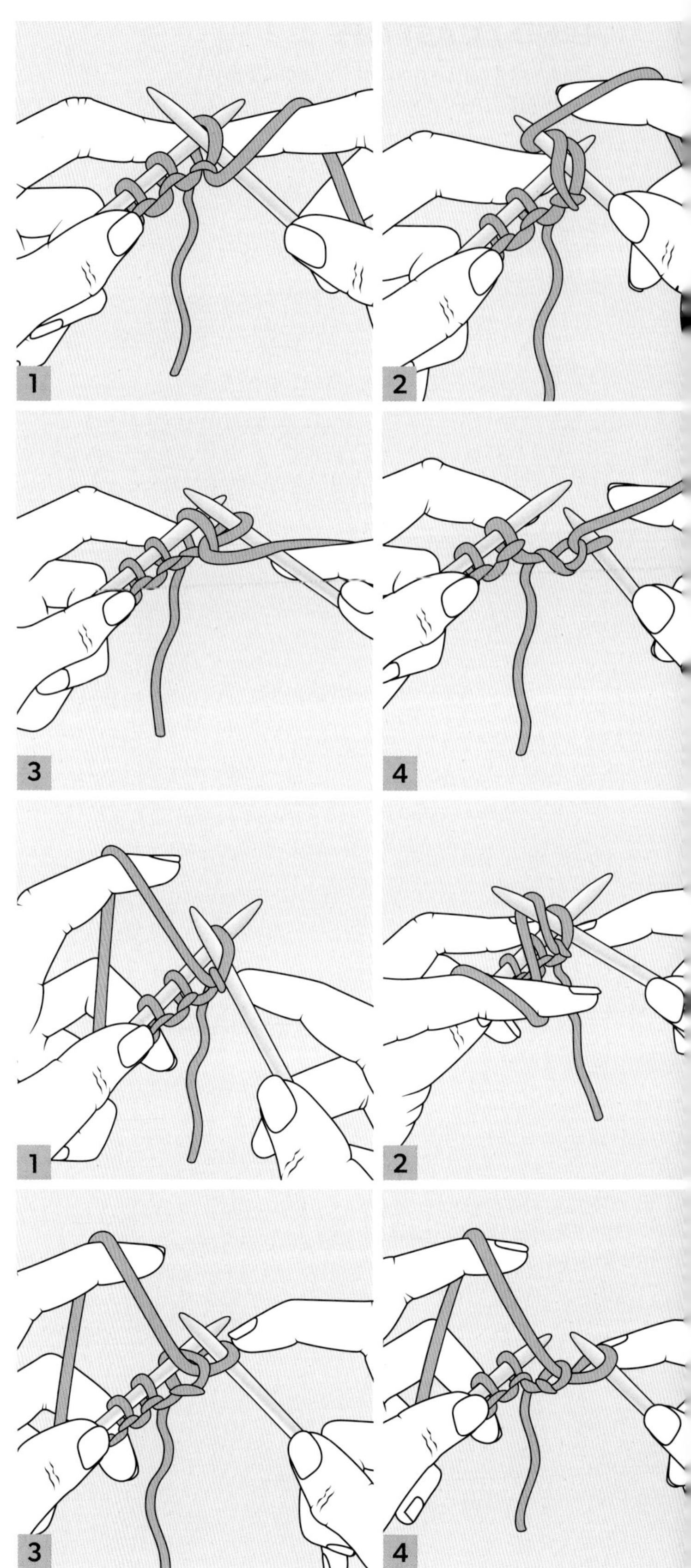

BIND / CAST OFF

Binding off can be done knitwise or purlwise, or following a pattern such as in rib.

1. To bind off knitwise, knit the first stitch, then knit a second stitch. Insert the tip of the left-hand needle into the first stitch.
2. Use the needle to lift the first stitch over the second stitch.
3. This binds off the first stitch. Knit the next stitch and then lift the previous stitch over it.

Repeat these steps until the row is bound off and there is just one stitch left. Break the yarn, thread it through the final stitch and tighten.

To bind off purlwise, work the same way as for knitwise but purl all the stitches instead of knitting them.

To bind off in rib, work the same way as for knitwise but knit all knit stitches and purl all purl stitches.

YARN OVER BIND / CAST OFF

This bind off gives a very stretchy edge, which is ideal for brioche knitting.

1. Knit the first stitch on the left-hand needle as normal, then bring the yarn to the front and take it over the needle to the back ready for the next stitch.
2. Knit the second stitch on the left-hand needle. Insert the tip of the left-hand needle into the yarn over and the stitch to the right and lift them both over the second stitch on the right-hand needle.
3. This binds off one stitch. Repeat steps 1 and 2 until the row is bound off and there is just one stitch left. Break the yarn, thread it through the final stitch and tighten.

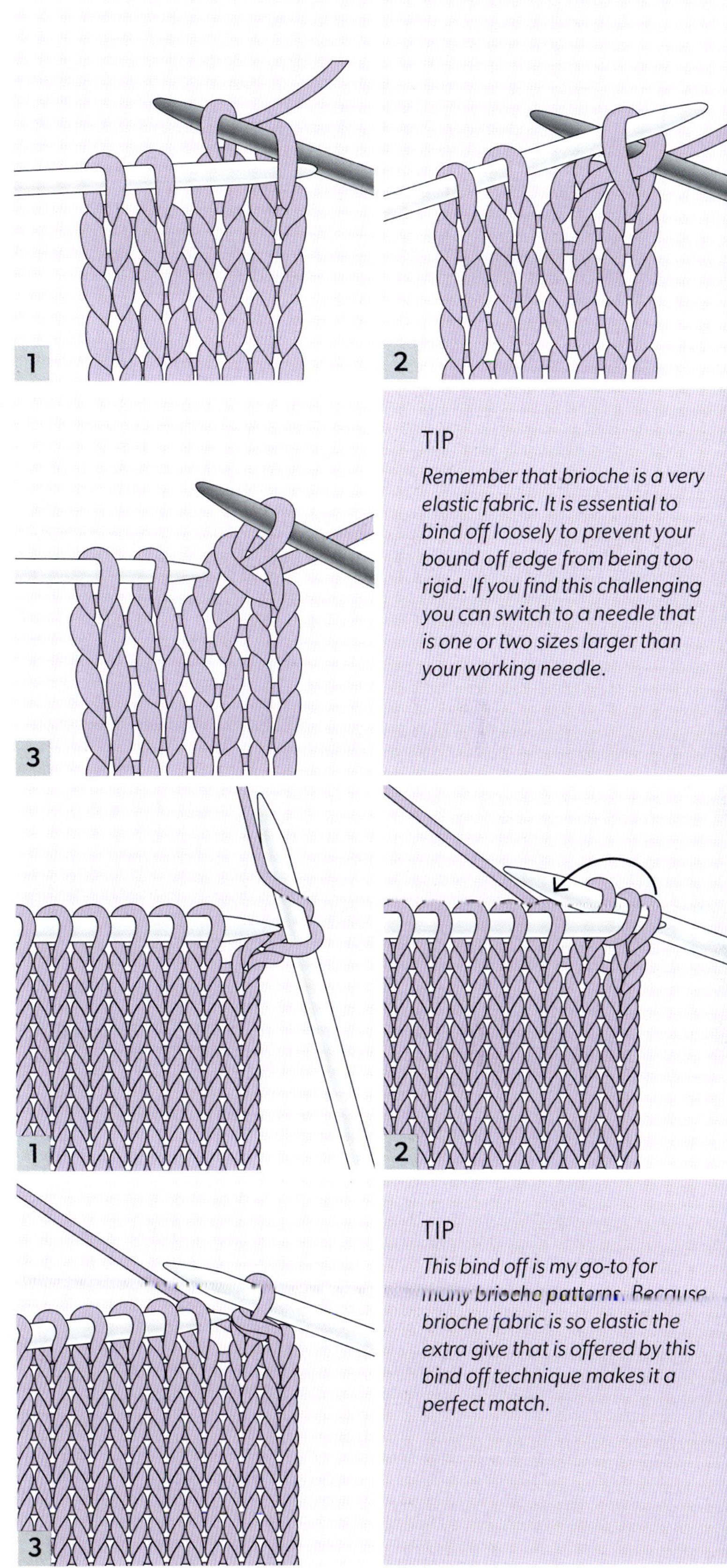

TIP

Remember that brioche is a very elastic fabric. It is essential to bind off loosely to prevent your bound off edge from being too rigid. If you find this challenging you can switch to a needle that is one or two sizes larger than your working needle.

TIP

This bind off is my go-to for many brioche patterns. Because brioche fabric is so elastic the extra give that is offered by this bind off technique makes it a perfect match.

KNIT TWO STITCHES TOGETHER (K2TOG)

This decreases by one stitch knitwise and makes a right-slanting decrease.

1. Insert the tip of the right-hand needle into the next two stitches from left to right and knit them as one stitch.

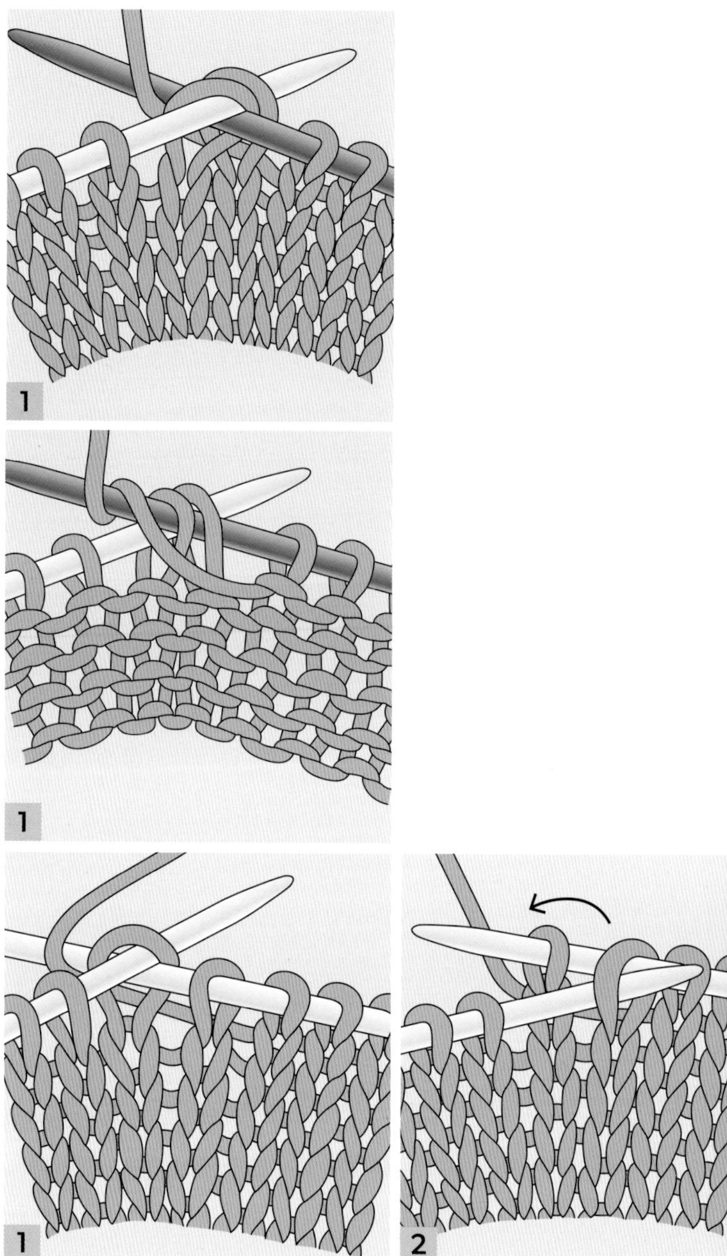

PURL TWO STITCHES TOGETHER (P2TOG)

This decreases by one stitch purlwise and makes a right-slanting decrease as viewed from the purl side of the work (left-slanting when viewed from the knit side of the work).

1. Insert the tip of the right-hand needle into the next two stitches from right to left and purl them as one stitch.

SLIP ONE, KNIT ONE, PASS SLIPPED STITCH OVER (SL1, K1, PSSO)

Usually worked two or three stitches in from an edge, this decreases by one stitch and makes a left-slanting decrease.

1. Slip the first stitch knitwise and then knit the second stitch as usual.
2. Use the tip of the left-hand needle to pass the slipped stitch over the knitted stitch.

SLIP ONE, KNIT TWO TOGETHER, PASS SLIPPED STITCH OVER (SL1, K2TOG, PSSO)

This technique decreases by two stitches at a time.

1. Using the tip of the needle, slip the first stitch onto the right-hand needle.
2. Insert the tip of the right-hand needle into the next two stitches from left to right and knit them as one stitch.
3. Pass the slipped stitch over the two stitches knitted together.

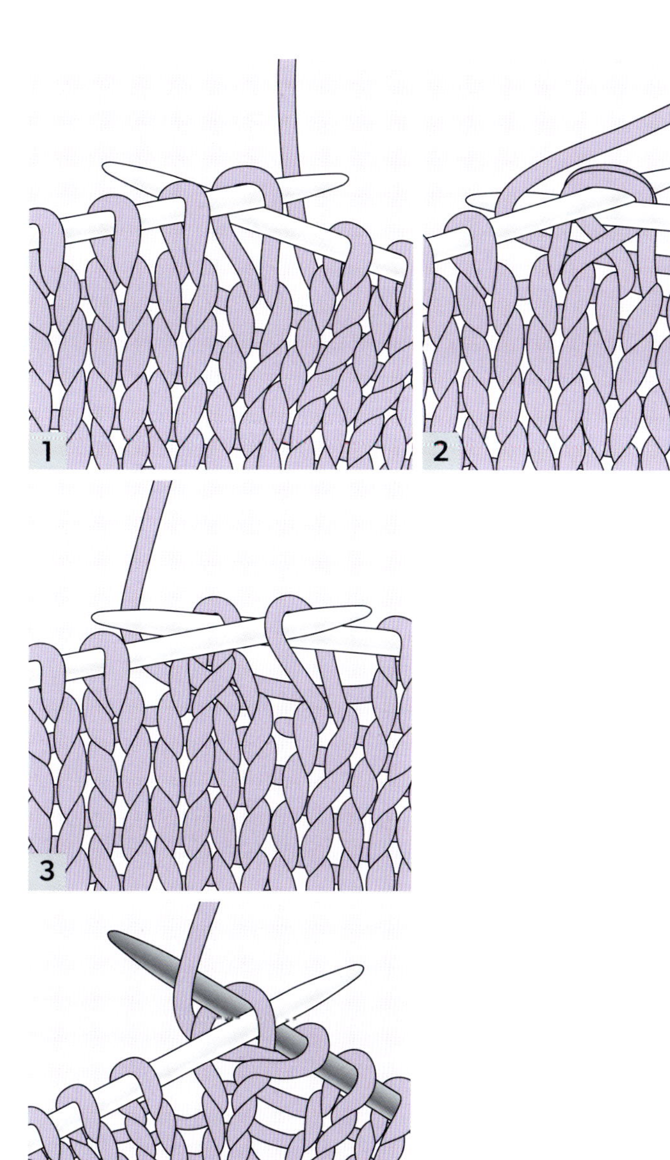

KNIT FRONT AND BACK (KFB)

This is a basic method of increasing one stitch knitwise, which is sometimes just abbreviated to inc. The increases will be visible.

1. Insert the tip of the right-hand needle into the stitch and knit it in the usual way but do not slide it off the needle. Insert the tip of the right-hand needle into the back of the same stitch on the left-hand needle, take the yarn forward and knit the stitch again. Now slide the original stitch off the left-hand needle. The increase will show as a bar across the base of the second stitch, so it is easy to count increases.

PURL FRONT AND BACK (PFB)

This is worked in the same ways as kfb, but working purl stitches instead of knit.

KNIT, YARN OVER, KNIT (KYOK)

This technique is a double increase that turns one stitch into three stitches.

1. Knit into the next stitch as normal, but do not slip the stitch off the left-hand needle.
2. Take the yarn around the right-hand needle as normal to create a yarn over.
3. Knit into the original stitch again, and this time slide it off the left-hand needle.
4. This completes the double increase stitch.

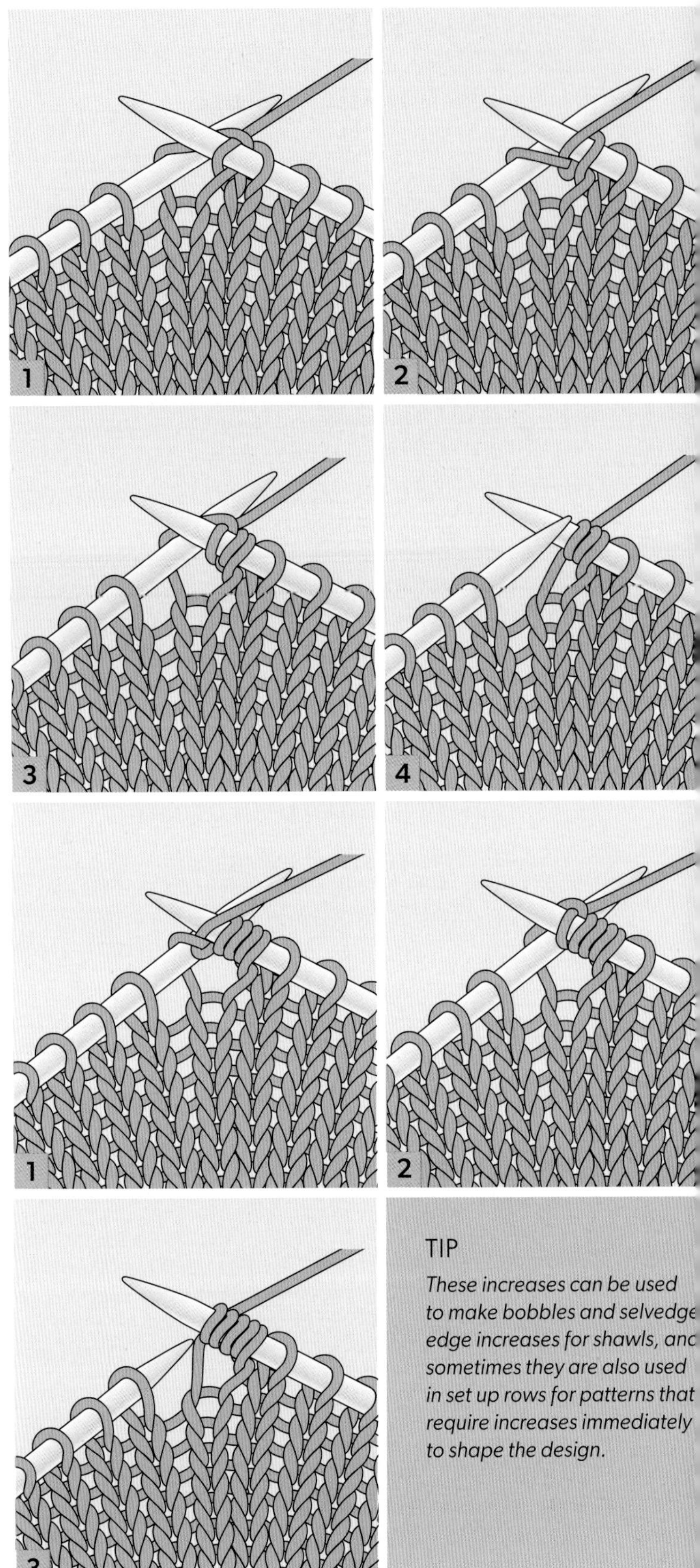

KNIT, YARN OVER, KNIT, YARN OVER, KNIT (KYOKYOK)

This technique is a quadruple increase that turns one stitch into a five-stitch bobble.

1. Follow steps 1 to 3 of KYOK, but do not slide the original stitch off the left-hand needle at the end. Take the yarn around the right-hand needle again as normal to create a yarn over.
2. Knit into the original stitch a third time, and this time slide it off the left-hand needle.
3. This completes the quadruple increase stitch.

TIP

These increases can be used to make bobbles and selvedge edge increases for shawls, and sometimes they are also used in set up rows for patterns that require increases immediately to shape the design.

KITCHENER STITCH / GRAFTING

Used to join two sets of live stitches in places where you do not want a seam.

1. With right side facing, hold the stitches evenly on two needles held parallel, with both tips to the right. Thread a darning needle with the yarn end and insert it purlwise through the first stitch on the front needle. Leave the stitch on the front needle
2. Pull the yarn through the stitch, then insert the darning needle knitwise through the first stitch on the back needle, again leaving the stitch on the needle.
3. Pull the yarn through and then insert the darning needle knitwise through the same stitch on the front needle.
4. Allow the first stitch on the front needle to drop, then insert the darning needle purlwise through the next stitch on the front needle.
5. Insert the darning needle purlwise through the same stitch on the back needle and slip it off the needle. Then insert the darning needle knitwise into the next stitch on the back needle.
6. Repeat steps 3 to 5 until all the stitches are grafted together.

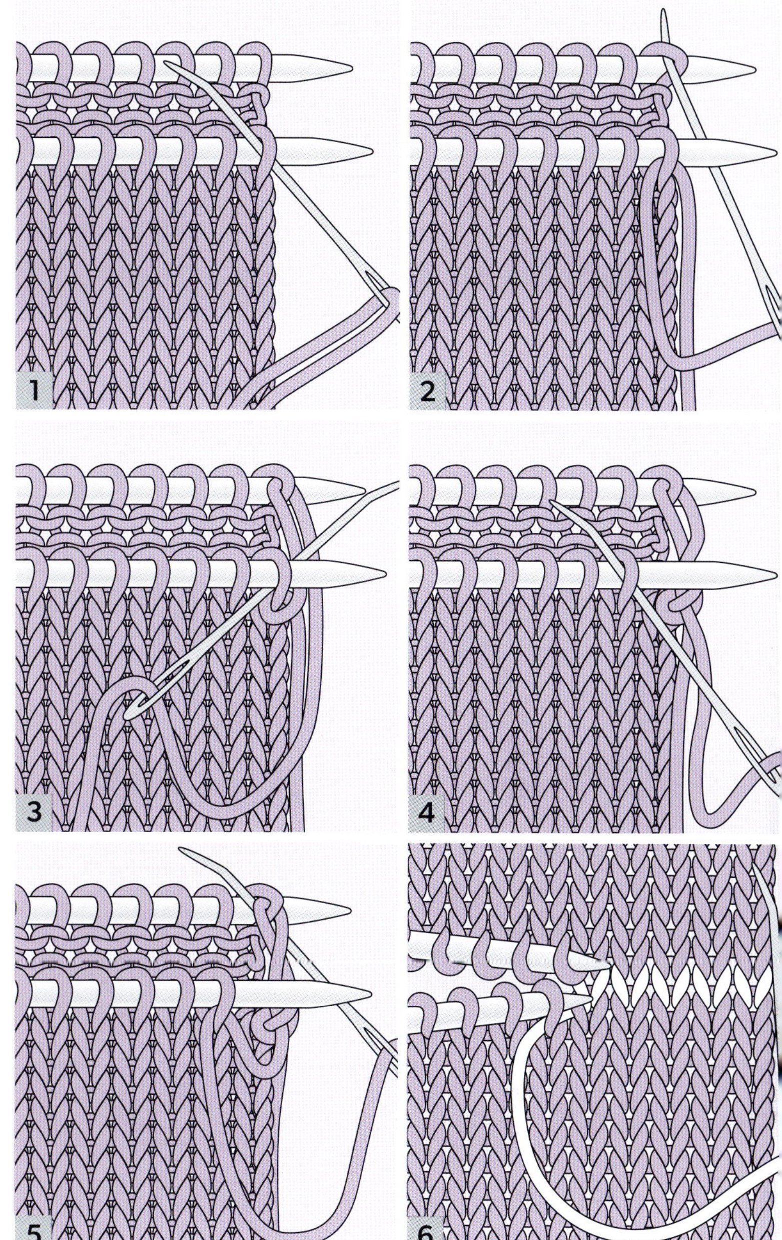

AFTERTHOUGHT HEEL

To work a heel at the end of a project, you need to pick up the stitches on either side of those made earlier in the waste yarn.

1. Slide a double-pointed needle through the right-hand leg of each stitch below the waste yarn stitches, from right to left.
2. Repeat with a second double-pointed needle, this time in the left-hand leg of the stitches above the waste yarn and working from left to right.
3. Remove the waste yarn stitches between the two needles.
4. Divide the picked up stitches equally between four double-pointed needles, ready to work the afterthought heel.

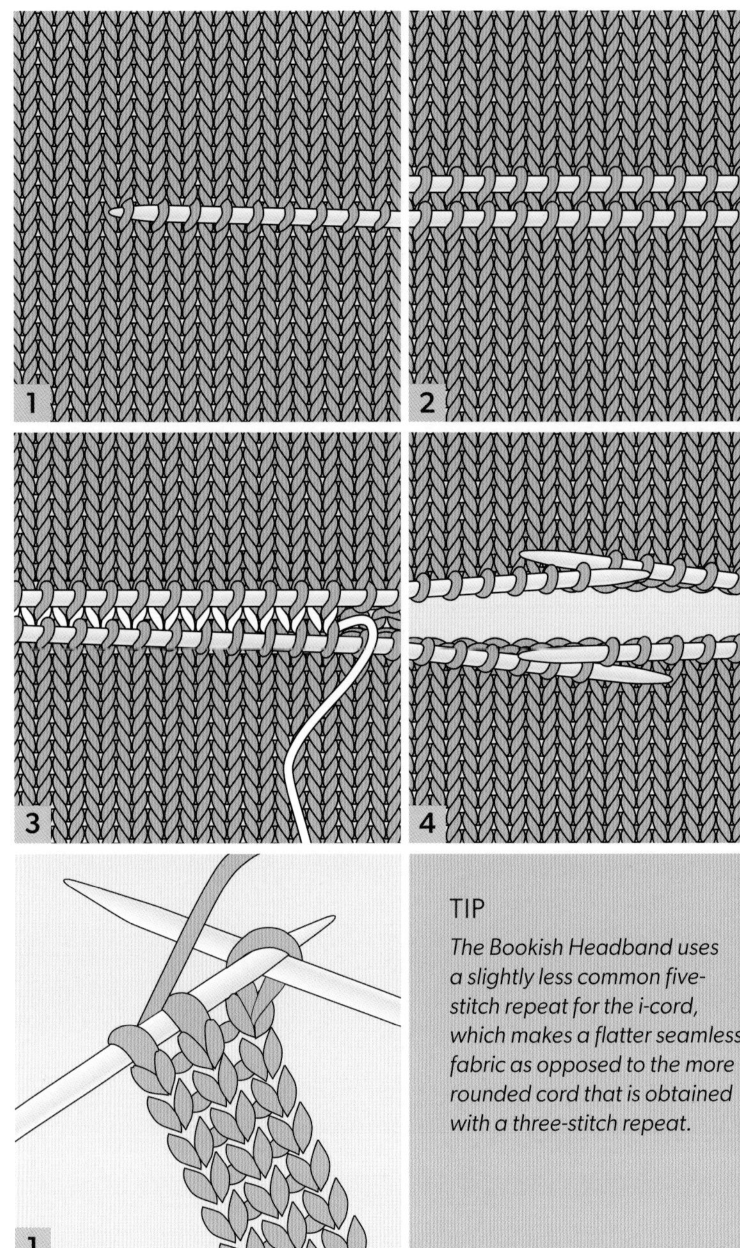

I-CORD

This is a knitted cord that is made by working a small number of stitches on double-pointed needles.

1. Cast on the number of stitches stated in the pattern, usually three, four or five. Knit to the end of the row, then slide the stitches to the other end of the needle and knit them again. Repeat this 'slide and knit again' sequence until the i-cord is the length that is required.

TIP

The Bookish Headband uses a slightly less common five-stitch repeat for the i-cord, which makes a flatter seamless fabric as opposed to the more rounded cord that is obtained with a three-stitch repeat.

ABBREVIATIONS

brk	Brioche knit: knit slipped stitch together with its yarn over
brkyobrk	A 2-stitch increase in brioche knit: brioche knit, yarn over, brioche knit into the same stitch
brLsl	A 2-stitch decrease that slants to the left, involving three stitches: slip the first stitch knitwise, brk the following two stitches together, pass the slipped stitch over
brp	Brioche purl: purl slipped stitch together with its yarn over
brpyobrp	A 2-stitch increase in brioche purl: brioche purl, yarn over, brioche purl into the same stitch
brRsl	A 2-stitch decrease that slants to the right, involving three stitches: slip the first stitch knitwise, knit the next stitch, pass the slipped stitch over, place stitch on left hand needle and pass the following stitch over. Place stitch back on right hand needle
CO	Cast on using the knit on method
k	Knit stitch
kfb	Knit into the front and back of the stitch to increase by 1 stitch
kyok	A 2-stitch increase: knit, yarn over, knit into the same stitch
kyokyok	A 4-stitch increase: knit, yarn over, knit, yarn over, knit into the same stitch
k2tog	Knit 2 stitches together to decrease by 1 stitch
k2togtbl	Knit 2 stitches together through the back loop to decrease by 1 stitch
k3tog	Knit 3 stitches together to decrease by 2 stitches
p	Purl stitch
pfb	Purl into front and back of stitch
PM / SM	Place marker / slide marker
psso	Pass slipped stitch over
sl1	Slip 1 stitch purlwise
sl1yo	With yarn in front, slip 1 stitch purlwise, yarn over
wyib / wyif	With yarn in back / with yarn in front
yo	Yarn over
[ ]	Repeat the sequence in brackets the number of times stated

YARN USED IN BOOK

West Wool - Tandem westwool.com
https://westwool.com

The Farmer's Daughter Fibers - Pishkun, Recollect Sport, Foxy Lady
https://thefarmersdaughterfibers.com

Malabrigo Yarn - Chunky, Rasta, Noventa
https://malabrigoyarn.com

Manos del Uruguay - Marla, Sami, Cardo
https://manos.uy/yarns

ABOUT THE AUTHOR

Lavanya Patricella is an American fiber artist, knitting instructor, knitwear designer, and photographer based in North Eastern Pennsylvania. She's been teaching knitting since 2010 and specializes in the captivating brioche stitch. Her hands-on approach to teaching and passion for the technique has consistently filled classes at local yarn shops and fiber festivals across the country. Lavanya has published more than 100 original patterns since 2014 both independently and in select publications. Beyond her creative endeavors Lavanya is a loving mother to three wonderful children and spends most of her free time immersed in her bountiful backyard garden, finding inspiration for her designs amidst nature's beauty.

THANKS

I'd like to dedicate this book to my three children, Tenzin, Tashi, and Vita. Thanks for understanding when I say "Let Mommy finish this last row."

Thanks to: Rosalie, my Gram for teaching me to knit; my family, for raising me to be me; my husband Harley for assisting with the photography for this book; Stephen West for introducing me to the brioche stitch and being such an amazing friend; the teams at Manos del Uruguay, Malabrigo Yarn, The Farmer's Daughter Fibers, and West Wool for the yarn support; all the yarn shops who have hosted and knitters who have taken my classes. And last but not least, the team at David & Charles for making this book a reality.

INDEX

A DAVID AND CHARLES BOOK
© David and Charles, Ltd 2024

David and Charles is an imprint of David and Charles, Ltd
Suite A, Tourism House, Pynes Hill, Exeter, EX2 5WS

Text and Designs © Lavanya Patricella 2024
Layout and Photography © David and Charles, Ltd 2024

First published in the UK and USA in 2024

Lavanya Patricella has asserted her right to be identified as author of this work in accordance with the Copyright, Designs and Patents Act, 1988.

All rights reserved. No part of this publication may be reproduced in any form or by any means, electronic or mechanical, by photocopying, recording or otherwise, without prior permission in writing from the publisher.

Readers are permitted to reproduce any of the designs in this book for their personal use and without the prior permission of the publisher. However, the designs in this book are copyright and must not be reproduced for resale.

The author and publisher have made every effort to ensure that all the instructions in the book are accurate and safe, and therefore cannot accept liability for any resulting injury, damage or loss to persons or property, however it may arise.

Names of manufacturers and product ranges are provided for the information of readers, with no intention to infringe copyright or trademarks.

A catalogue record for this book is available from the British Library.

ISBN-13: 9781446313718 paperback
ISBN-13: 9781446313732 EPUB
ISBN-13: 9781446313725 PDF

This book has been printed on paper from approved suppliers and made from pulp from sustainable sources.

Printed in China through Asia Pacific Offset for:
David and Charles, Ltd
Suite A, Tourism House, Pynes Hill, Exeter, EX2 5WS

10 9 8 7 6 5 4 3 2 1

Publishing Director: Ame Verso
Senior Commissioning Editor: Sarah Callard
Publishing Manager: Jeni Chown
Editor: Victoria Allen
Project Editors: Sam Winkler and Marie Clayton
Lead Designer: Sam Staddon
Designer: Nikki Ellis
Pre-press Designer: Susan Reansbury
Illustrations: Kuo Kang Chen
Photography and Styling: Lavanya Patricella
Production Manager: Beverley Richardson

David and Charles publishes high-quality books on a wide range of subjects. For more information visit www.davidandcharles.com.

Share your makes with us on social media using #dandcbooks and follow us on Facebook and Instagram by searching for @dandcbooks.

Layout of the digital edition of this book may vary depending on reader hardware and display settings.